THE ULTIMATE
Wizarding World
PUZZLE BOOK

Reveal the Secrets of Hogwarts and Harry Potter

Media Lab Books
For inquiries, contact customerservice@topixmedia.com

Copyright 2024 Topix Media Lab

Published by Topix Media Lab
14 Wall Street, Suite 3C
New York, NY 10005

PRINTED IN CHINA

ISBN-13: 978-1-956403-67-1
ISBN-10: 1-956403-67-1

CEO Tony Romando

Vice President & Publisher Phil Sexton
Senior Vice President of Sales & New Markets Tom Mifsud
Vice President of Retail Sales & Logistics Linda Greenblatt
Vice President of Manufacturing & Distribution Nancy Puskuldjian
Digital Marketing & Strategy Manager Elyse Gregov

Chief Content Officer Jeff Ashworth
Senior Acquisitions Editor Noreen Henson
Creative Director Susan Dazzo
Photo Director Dave Weiss
Executive Editor Tim Baker
Managing Editor Tara Sherman

Content Editor Tim Baker
Content Designer Alyssa Bredin Quirós
Features Editor Trevor Courneen
Associate Editor Juliana Sharaf
Designers Glen Karpowich, Mikio Sakai
Copy Editor & Fact Checker Madeline Raynor
Assistant Photo Editor Jenna Addesso
Assistant Managing Editor Claudia Acevedo

MuggleNet
The #1 Wizarding World Resource Since 1999

Creative & Marketing Director Kat Miller

Special thanks to MuggleNet staff for the following features:

"Did You Know?" trivia (throughout) Aly Kirk, Amanda Halmes, Carolyn Sehgal, Marica Laing, Richa Venkatraman and Victoria Durgin

Your O.W.L. Exams (pgs. 142-149)
Marica Laing, Marissa Osman, Rex Hadden, Richa Venkatraman and Victoria Durgin

The Half-Blood Prince's Textbook (pgs. 188-189)
Carolyn Sehgal, Jennifer Creevy, John L. Wilda, Kimira V. Leonard and Sas Rhodes

Your N.E.W.T. Exams (pgs. 198-204)
Elizabeth Pease, Marissa Osman, Rex Hadden and Richa Venkatraman

Fact checking by Catherine Lai

1C-B24-1

A Wizarding Test

FOR MORE THAN two decades, the wondrous wizarding world of *Harry Potter* has inspired imaginations around the world, building a fan base larger than perhaps any other fictional property. In the following pages, the experts at MuggleNet offer the ultimate challenge for millions of loyal readers: *The Ultimate Wizarding World Puzzle Book*. Packed with unique ways for you to test your wizarding world knowledge, it's sure to keep you occupied whether you're killing time aboard the Hogwarts Express or taking a break from studying for your O.W.L.s. Test your knowledge of the entire *Harry Potter* saga with expert-level trivia, mazes, wizarding games, codebreaking and much, much more!

CONTENTS

YEAR ONE

HARRY POTTER

and the

SORCERER'S STONE

How well do you know the ins and outs
of our first look at the wizarding world?

First-years approach Hogwarts by boat in *Harry Potter and the Sorcerer's Stone* (2001).

Find Your Wizarding Wares

Based on your knowledge of the wizarding world, can you fill in the names of the missing Diagon Alley businesses on the map below?

A wand chooses a wizard here.

3

A tavern that features the entrance to Diagon Alley in its yard.

1

4

Where Harry first sets his eyes on a Nimbus 2000.

2

This alliterative business sells frozen treats.

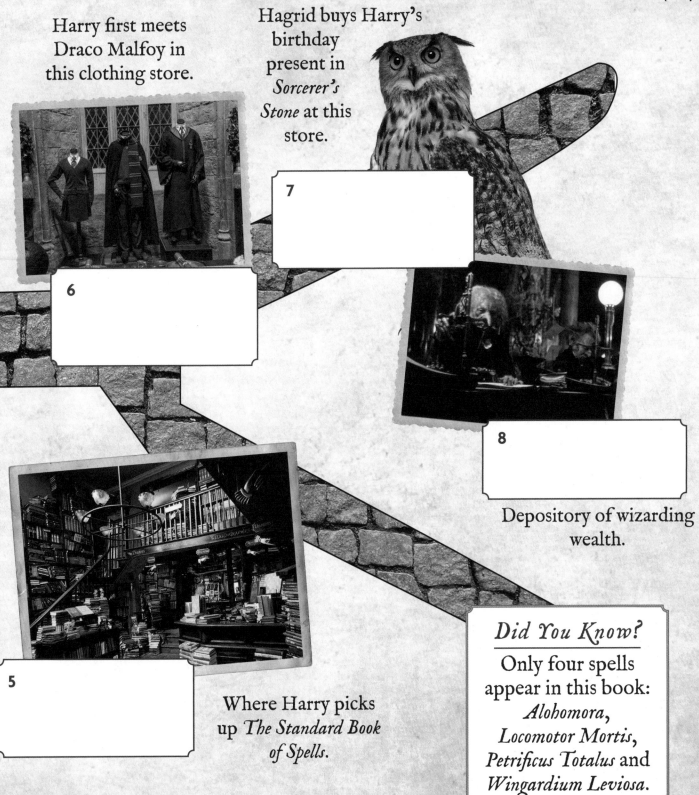

Clockwise from top left: Daniel Radcliffe as Harry Potter and John Hurt as Ollivander in *Harry Potter and the Sorcerer's Stone* (2001); Slytherin costumes on display; Gringotts goblins in *Harry Potter and the Sorcerer's Stone* (2001); Daniel Radcliffe as Harry and Kenneth Branagh as Gilderoy Lockhart in *Harry Potter and the Chamber of Secrets* (2002).

Harry first meets Draco Malfoy in this clothing store.

Hagrid buys Harry's birthday present in *Sorcerer's Stone* at this store.

7

6

8

5

Depository of wizarding wealth.

Where Harry picks up *The Standard Book of Spells*.

Did You Know?

Only four spells appear in this book: *Alohomora*, *Locomotor Mortis*, *Petrificus Totalus* and *Wingardium Leviosa*.

Did You Know?

When a Gringotts curse fills a vault with multiplying treasure that burns to the touch, Hermione casts *Impervius* to save the day.

Warwick Davis as a Gringotts teller in *Harry Potter and the Sorcerer's Stone* (2001).

A Robbery at Gringotts

Thieves have broken into the Diagon Alley institution and made off with treasures of immense value. Can you help the bank's goblin employees figure out what else has been stolen?

The total amount stolen was valued at 144,000 Galleons. Of the 12 items stolen, seven of them have already been figured to be worth a total of 72,000 Galleons.

INVENTORY LIST

12,750 Galleons	Antique Foe-Glass
4,990 Galleons	Goblin-Made Dagger
16,840 Galleons	Jeweled Pensieve
19,000 Galleons	Gold Ingots
26,850 Galleons	Signed First Edition, *Quidditch Through the Ages*
8,050 Galleons	Original Pressing, Merlin Chocolate Frog Card
14,360 Galleons	Solid Gold Omnioculars
20,000 Galleons	Uncut Sapphires, Rubies and Opals

Can you use addition, subtraction and the vault's remaining inventory (provided) to determine which five additional items were taken?

1. _____   4. _____

2. _____   5. _____

3. _____

Hogwarts Class of '98

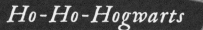

Ho-Ho-Hogwarts

What did Godric Gryffindor call the potions he made?

GRYFFIN-DRAUGHTS.

The Hogwarts Great Hall seen in the *Harry Potter* films, pictured, is modeled after the Great Hall at Christ Church in Oxford, England.

COLLECTION CHRISTOPHEL/ALAMY

CAN YOU REMEMBER THE HOUSES INTO WHICH EACH MEMBER OF HARRY'S YEAR IS SORTED?

Daphne Greengrass   _____

Seamus Finnigan   _____

Parvati Patil   _____

Draco Malfoy   _____

Vincent Crabbe   _____

Ernie Macmillan   _____

Justin Finch-Fletchley   _____

Wayne Hopkins   _____

Hannah Abbott   _____

Susan Bones   _____

Anthony Goldstein   _____

Lavender Brown   _____

Michael Corner   _____

Terry Boot   _____

Dean Thomas   _____

Padma Patil   _____

Mandy Brocklehurst   _____

Lisa Turpin   _____

Hermione Granger   _____

Harry Potter   _____

Gregory Goyle   _____

Theodore Nott   _____

Neville Longbottom   _____

Blaise Zabini   _____

Pansy Parkinson   _____

Ron Weasley   _____

Millicent Bulstrode   _____

G
Gryffindor

H
Hufflepuff

R
Ravenclaw

S
Slytherin

Changing Stairs

Can you navigate the fickle staircases of Hogwarts and make your way back to the common room?

Hogwarts's changing staircases as depicted in *Harry Potter and the Sorcerer's Stone* (2001).

COLLECTION CHRISTOPHEL/ALAMY

START

END

Hogwarts Curriculum

YEAR ONE

Can you find the words and phrases that proved crucial
for Harry's first-year studies at Hogwarts?

1. This creature, also a failing O.W.L.
and N.E.W.T. grade, causes a
panic at Halloween.

_____

2. This spell is used by Hermione in
the film to fix Harry's glasses on
the Hogwarts Express.

_____

3. Hermione and Ron plan to use this
"leg-locker" curse on Professor Snape
if he attempts to harm Harry
during a Quidditch match.

_____

4. Hermione chides Ron for
not being able to properly
pronounce this levitation charm.

_____

5. This stone, found in a goat's
stomach, is used in potions.

_____

6. This potion ingredient is also
known as monkshood and aconite.

_____

7. Making his way through the Forbidden
Forest with Hagrid, Harry meets members
of this horse hybrid species.

_____

8. Hagrid's trusty canine companion,
Fang, is described in the
books as what breed?

_____

9. Professor Quirrell, supposedly
afraid of attack from vampires, wears a
necklace of this fragrant vegetable.

_____

```
M G Y E U P S R H B M L T R O L L
Y Q A C F Q X Y E C J V D J P D O
D A W H P E D B W B M Y B L A J R
Q K H F N O B L J W E M Z C U Z A
W C Z M U D D J R U D I H M F O Y
W R L V Y U W I S A E B I F H P A
T I J T L C L K V X W G X Q G U
G S N L P D F O Z C E N T A U R U
L Y B G V J B L Y A Q P G F V S K
O M O T A R N X N O B O G G A A C
C S J D K R H W S I L C S K H C S
O B H M R D X J W U U D P U E M
M H G P J W K I Z X Y L D Q Y Z R
O E A M Z O Q K U P B U C Q I A T
T Y R N B L X I Z M Q S B A H H J
O X L F O F V S I Y L R K G Y H I
R Q I B A S I G I F B E L W S M S
M Y C E R B D E Q H U P V F A L C
O F H Z H A A L N W W A W I F I A
R I H O O N A H B B J R U V O U M
T J D A U E S H J A A O X U R S D
I Z K R N Z R P A Q I H D Q T N A
S W N L D A Y B E P R K G M R J N
```

Hogwarts Curriculum

Continued

YEAR ONE

How closely were you paying attention to the *Harry Potter* books and films?

1. Scenes in the Hogwarts library's restricted section were filmed at which historic U.K. university?
  A. Cambridge
  B. The London School of Economics
  C. Oxford
  D. St. Andrews

2. What does the inscription above the Mirror of Erised say?

_____

3. Three "actors," named Gizmo, Ook and Sprout, shared which role in *Harry Potter and the Sorcerer's Stone?*
  A. Hedwig
  B. Scabbers
  C. Mrs. Norris
  D. Errol

4. Beginning with *Sorcerer's Stone*, Daniel Radcliffe went through 160 of these while filming the series.
  A. Wands
  B. Robes
  C. Broomsticks
  D. Pairs of glasses

5. Astute viewers might notice a trophy "for services to Hogwarts" won by this student next to a Quidditch award during Harry's detention scene.

_____

6. This character, played by Rik Mayall, was cut from the film and never revisited in the series.

_____

7. What kind of sandwiches does Mrs. Weasley pack for Ron's journey to Hogwarts, forgetting he doesn't like them?

_____

8. Where does the first act of Transfiguration we see performed by Professor McGonagall in the film take place?

_____

9. Ron uses *Wingardium Leviosa* successfully for the first time on which holiday evening?

_____

Daniel Radcliffe as Harry Potter.

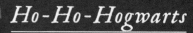

Ho-Ho-Hogwarts

What does Professor Flitwick have in common with his little teapot?

THEY'RE BOTH SHORT AND STOUT.

Hogwarts Curriculum

Continued

YEAR ONE

How closely were you paying attention to the *Harry Potter* books and films?

10. What is the first treat Harry tastes off the Hogwarts Express trolley?

_____

11. In the book, which character gave Harry each of these Christmas presents during his first year?
  A. A 50-pence piece _____
  B. Homemade fudge and a sweater _____
  C. Chocolate Frogs _____
  D. Wooden flute _____
  E. Invisibility cloak _____

12. Though it's cast nonverbally, the first spell Harry sees in *Harry Potter and the Sorcerer's Stone* is a Transfiguration spell that changes the appearance of which character?

_____

Ho-Ho-Hogwarts

How do Hogwarts students send secret messages?

WITH OWL-GORITHMIC ENCRYPTION.

13. The Gryffindor first-years watch Professor McGonagall turn her desk into a _____ during their first Transfiguration lesson.

14. Ron, first unable to master the incantation, uses this levitation spell to save Hermione from a giant troll. _____

15. This spell used by Hermione to get into the third floor corridor is also known as the "Thief's Friend." _____

16. Neville is the first character to be hit with a full body bind, signified by which incantation? _____

Plotting the Plot

Can you match the
chapter name to what
happened in it?

Chapter Name

1. __ The Boy Who Lived
2. __ Diagon Alley
3. __ The Sorting Hat
4. __ The Mirror of Erised
5. __ The Forbidden Forest
6. __ The Man With Two Faces

What Occurred

A. Harry becomes a member of Gryffindor House.

B. Harry is dropped off on his aunt
   and uncle's doorstep.

C. During detention with Hagrid, Harry
   encounters Voldemort.

D. Harry is introduced to the wizarding world.

E. Harry stops Quirrell from stealing
   the Sorcerer's Stone.

F. Harry sees his deepest heart's desire.

Wizarding Words

Can you find the magical words hidden in the puzzle opposite?

Rupert Grint as Ron Weasley and Daniel Radcliffe as Harry Potter in *Harry Potter and the Sorcerer's Stone* (2001).

WORD BANK

Alchemy
Basilisk
Bezoar
Hexes
Leprechaun
Mandrake
Poltergeist
Spellbook
Wandlore
Werewolf

```
B L S H N W Y S Z P Z Y J B A B F
D G A Z E P B K V O P Z K F H M Z
C Q D K C U H O A M I U K N B A R
G Q M E S R Q E O B V B J X E I Y
L Q N N K J O I X C T B E Z O A R
L Y S Q W I L E R E Y K D Y T O N
I S L I M E R O A E S U E Q Z M R
V H E R A O R Y E I Z D M S B E M
G N P P N B W E O M J K U N G X U
T V R I D A W A W Y L P W N O H G
X Q E W R L P W S O V J T T B F E
Q C C Y A C A C Q X L W K L A U L
K T H P K H S B I W D F E K S M O
S U A F E E X K C H F X O N I I H
W P U Z H M J V J T C S D T L H Z
P A N E D Y P O L T E R G E I S T
F T N P V Z E B T T Y Z J R S Y B
Y W M D D M N C Q Y A N W K K G V
N W U Y L A A Q R T G M H H R D Z
A D V W F O T U L J M N L D Y E W
X E A J T K R N L Q K R J O M M K
B H V A V C W E P S E S Q A S K I
Q S P E L L B O O K X Y O S N Q V
```

Be the Sorting Hat

Based on their attributes, can you Sort the following students into the correct Hogwarts House?

NAME Gwinnifer Gaines

RESIDENCE Gaines Manor, Fife, Scotland

FAVORITE SCHOOL SUBJECT History of Magic—the pageant of noble pureblood wizards of old makes her yearn for a better, simpler time.

BIGGEST AMBITION AT HOGWARTS To attach her name to as many accomplishments and records as possible so no one will forget her name.

IDEAL VACATION Semester-long exchange program with Durmstrang

FRIENDS DESCRIBE HER AS Calculating, Isolated, Focused

NAME William B. Snidely

RESIDENCE Mayfair, London, England

FAVORITE SCHOOL SUBJECT Herbology, as both his Muggle parents are florists and it feels familiar.

BIGGEST AMBITION FOR HOGWARTS To help his friends earn the House Cup.

IDEAL VACATION Tapas Tour of Spain

FRIENDS DESCRIBE HIM AS Affable, Understanding, Capable

NAME Edwina Runkle

RESIDENCE Ottery St. Catchpole, England

FAVORITE SCHOOL SUBJECT Defense Against the Dark Arts—She's wanted to be in Magical Law Enforcement since her Auror aunt was killed in the Wizarding Wars.

BIGGEST AMBITION FOR HOGWARTS To become Head Girl.

IDEAL VACATION Time off? She'd rather shadow someone at the Ministry of Magic to earn valuable experience.

FRIENDS DESCRIBE HER AS Loyal, Intelligent, Fearless

NAME Shep Holbrook

RESIDENCE Cardiff, Wales

FAVORITE SCHOOL SUBJECT Potions—anyone can be a master potion-maker if they follow the directions to a T.

BIGGEST AMBITION AT HOGWARTS To earn the highest possible marks on all of his N.E.W.T.s, setting himself up for a stellar career.

IDEAL VACATION A week-long pass to the restricted section of the Hogwarts Library.

FRIENDS DESCRIBE HIM AS Sardonic, Bookish, Easily Bored

The Sorting Hat.

Daniel Radcliffe as Harry Potter and Tom Felton as Draco Malfoy in *Harry Potter and the Sorcerer's Stone* (2001).

TCD/PROD.DB/ALAMY

The Forbidden Forest

Harry is serving detention in the Forbidden Forest with Draco Malfoy and Fang. Can you lead them out of the woods?

START

END

Wandlore Wisdom

As a first-year, Harry meets Ollivander, a man who never forgets a face or wand. Can you remember which wand belongs to whom?

Daniel Radcliffe as Harry Potter in *Harry Potter and the Sorcerer's Stone* (2001).

_____ **1.** 11" holly, phoenix feather, nice and supple. Known for its use of disarming spells.

_____ **2.** 10", hawthorn, unicorn hair, reasonably springy. Changes owners in Book Seven.

_____ **3.** 12", ash, unicorn hair. Splits in Book Two.

_____ **4.** 13½", yew, phoenix feather—Fawkes's feather, to be precise.

_____ **5.** 12¾", walnut, dragon heartstring, unyielding. Loses a duel to Molly Weasley.

_____ **6.** 10¾", vine, dragon heartstring. Used for ocular repair in the first film.

_____ **7.** 14", willow, unicorn hair. Used to stop a rainstorm in a Ministry of Magic office.

_____ **8.** 8", birch, dragon heartstring. Nearly performs an unforgivable curse on a Hogwarts student.

_____ **9.** 9¼ ", chestnut, dragon heartstring, brittle.

_____ **10.** 10¼ inches, hornbeam, dragon heartstring, quite rigid.

Magic Shadows

Can you tell which of the silhouettes opposite is a direct match?

Daniel Radcliffe as Harry Potter.

Ho-Ho-Hogwarts

How did the first-year win a Nimbus 2000?

IN A SWEEP-STAKES.

Teacher of the Year

1. Harry first meets Professor Quirrell in this wizarding locale:

_____

2. Quirrell's classroom is described as smelling like this plant:

_____

3. Quirrell claims to have gotten his turban from a prince for ridding his kingdom of which magical creature?
A. Sphinx   B. Boggart
C. Grindylow   D. Zombie

4. What is Professor Quirrell's first name?
A. Quintus   B. Quentin
C. Quirinus   D. Quarl

5. In the movie, Quirrell is holding an iguana when Professor McGonagall comes to his classroom to inquire about which student?

_____

6. What other subject did Quirrell teach at Hogwarts?
A. Arithmancy
B. None—he only ever taught DADA
C. Potions
D. Muggle Studies

7. What is Quirrell's wand core made of?
A. Dragon heartstring
B. Unicorn hair
C. Veela hair
D. Thestral hair

8. Where did Hagrid claim Quirrell had a run-in with a vampire?

_____

9. In the fourth book, which of the following adjectives does Voldemort NOT use to describe Quirrell as he reflects on their relationship?
A. Young   B. Gullible
C. Ambitious   D. Foolish

10. Under which of the following pretenses did Professor Quirrell claim to be in Diagon Alley when he first meets Harry?
A. Making a deposit at Gringotts
B. Buying a book on vampires
C. Having an ice cream at Florian Fortescue's
D. Having his robes tailored

Professor Quirrell

Checkmate Challenge

Can you end these games in one move and prove you're ready to play Gryffindor's best?

Emma Watson as Hermione Granger, Rupert Grint as Ron Weasley and Daniel Radcliffe as Harry Potter in *Harry Potter and the Sorcerer's Stone* (2001).

GRYFFINDOR'S RESIDENT chess master is tired of beating everyone all the time, so they've created some brain-building puzzles to help other members of the House hone their skills. Hopefully, after solving all of these, you'll be able to give the chess expert and their trusty old wizard chess set a decent challenge. Playing as white, can you reach checkmate in one move on each of the following boards?

1. _____

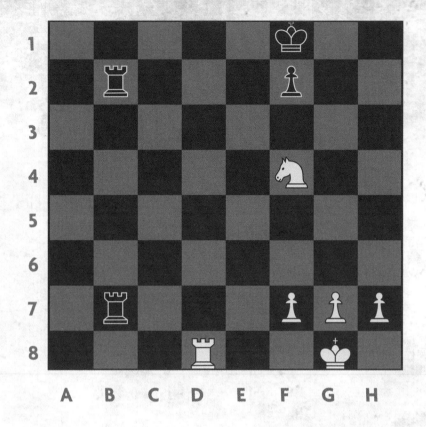

2. _____

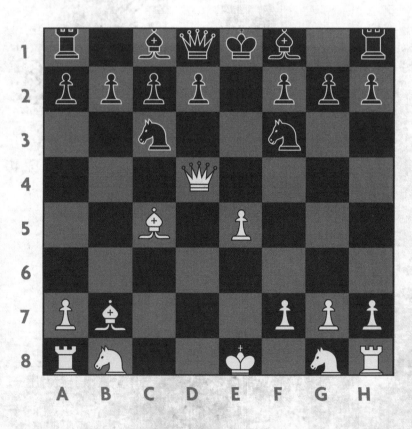

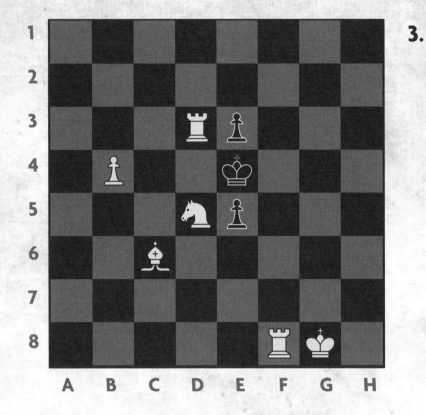

3. _____

4. _____

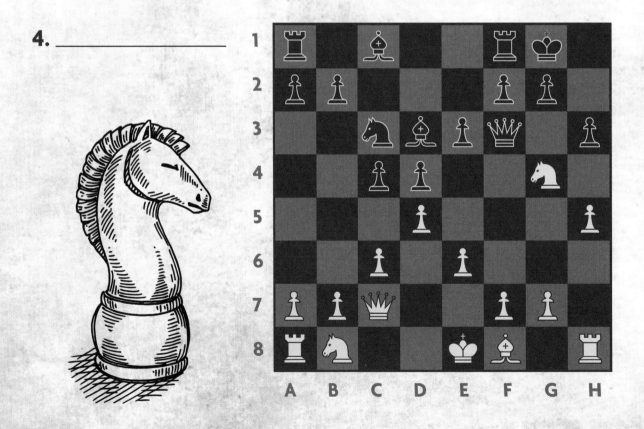

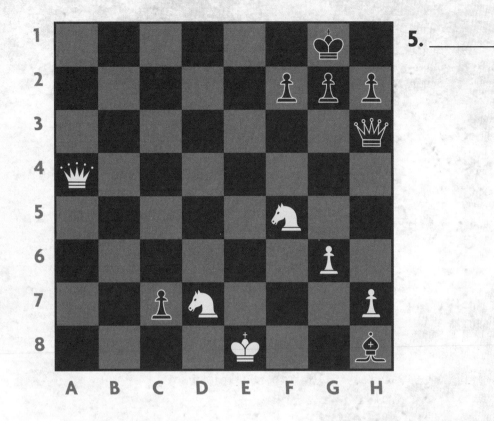

5. _____

6. _____

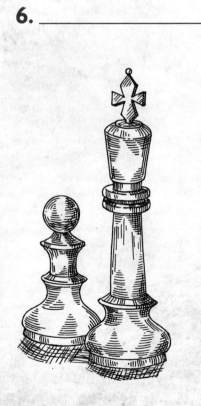

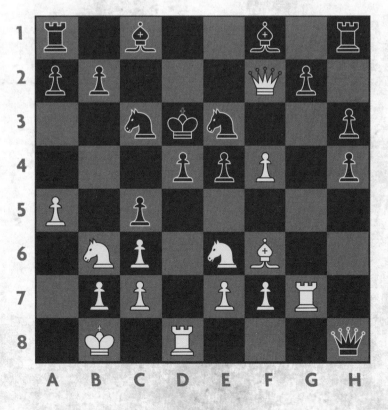

Zoë Wanamaker as
Madam Hooch teaches
first-year students how
to fly in *Harry Potter
and the Sorcerer's
Stone* (2001).

MuggleNet's Expert Trivia

YEAR ONE

You must have been paying close attention to every word of the saga if you can answer all of these questions.

1. Who was the first caretaker of Hogwarts?

_____

2. Which Hogwarts professor was named after their grandmother?

_____

3. Which Hogwarts professor directed Hogwarts's one and only Christmas play?

_____

4. Which broom did Madam Hooch learn to fly on?

_____

5. Which incantation is used to make something watertight?

_____

6. What is the incantation for the Tickling Charm?

_____

7. The Horton-Keitch Braking Charm was invented by the founders of which broom company?

_____

8. Which charm does Harry accidentally mix up with a color-changing charm during his practical O.W.L. exam?

_____

9. What is the charm incantation for keeping out Muggles in a targeted area?

_____

10. Which charm is required to eradicate an infestation of Bundimuns?

_____

Third-Floor Corridor

Can you make your way through Hogwarts to the off-limits corridor where Fluffy guards the Sorcerer's Stone?

Fluffy the three-headed dog in *Harry Potter and the Sorcerer's Stone* (2001).

START

END

YEAR TWO

HARRY POTTER
and the
CHAMBER OF SECRETS

The Heir of Slytherin is loose once again at Hogwarts.
And Harry, as usual, is caught in the middle.

The Flying Ford Anglia and the Hogwarts Express in *Harry Potter and the Chamber of Secrets* (2002).

New Friends, New Foes

Can you unscramble the names of the characters introduced in the second installment of the saga?

1. RGAAOG

_____

2. RAUHTR ALWSEYE

_____

3. LCONI EECVRY

_____

4. BOBYD

_____

5. TMO ERDIDL

_____

6. CULISU LAFYOM

_____

7. RM. OBGRNI

_____

8. NMAINOG YLRTME

_____

9. IGLEODRY LCOHRAKT

_____

Toby Jones provided the voice for Dobby in _Harry Potter and the Chamber of Secrets_ (2002).

Arthur Weasley's
Silly Circuits

Mr. Weasley, whom Harry meets in *Chamber of Secrets*, is notoriously fascinated with Muggle technology and has decided to start learning about electricity. Can you help him locate the correct piece to fill in his panel without causing a short circuit?

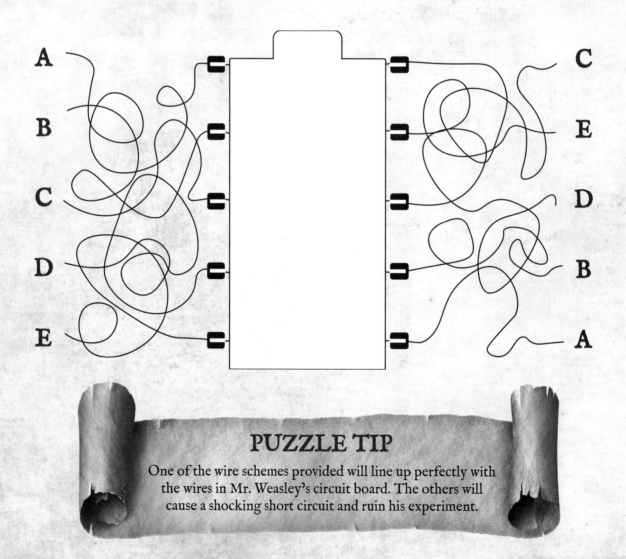

PUZZLE TIP

One of the wire schemes provided will line up perfectly with the wires in Mr. Weasley's circuit board. The others will cause a shocking short circuit and ruin his experiment.

The Weasleys visiting Bill in Egypt, where he is working for Gringotts.

Arthur Weasley's
Silly Circuits
Continued

Mr. Weasley is notoriously fascinated with Muggle technology and has decided to start learning about electricity. Can you help him locate the correct piece to fill in his panel without causing a short circuit?

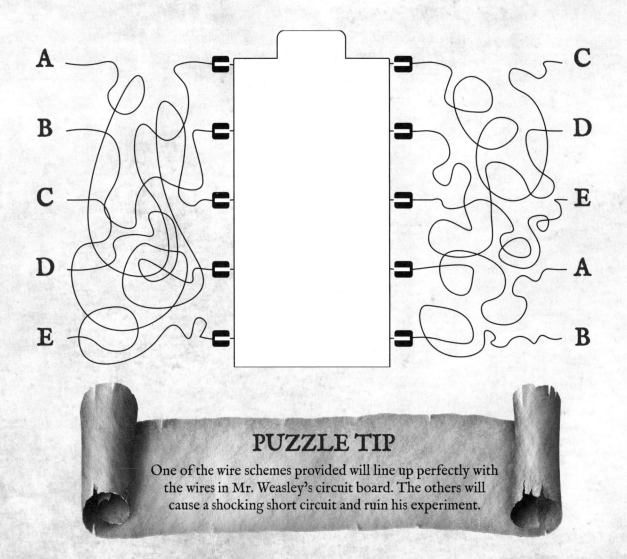

PUZZLE TIP

One of the wire schemes provided will line up perfectly with the wires in Mr. Weasley's circuit board. The others will cause a shocking short circuit and ruin his experiment.

Mark Willams as Arthur Weasley in *Harry Potter and the Deathly Hallows, Part 2* (2011).

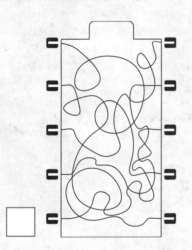

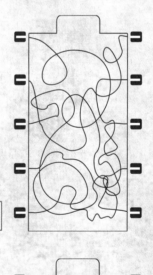

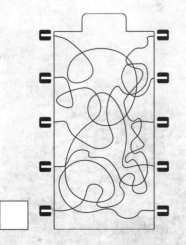

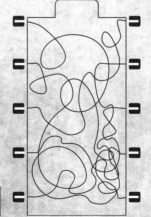

Arthur Weasley's
Silly Circuits
Continued

Mr. Weasley is notoriously fascinated with Muggle technology and has decided to start learning about electricity. Can you help him locate the correct piece to fill in his panel without causing a short circuit?

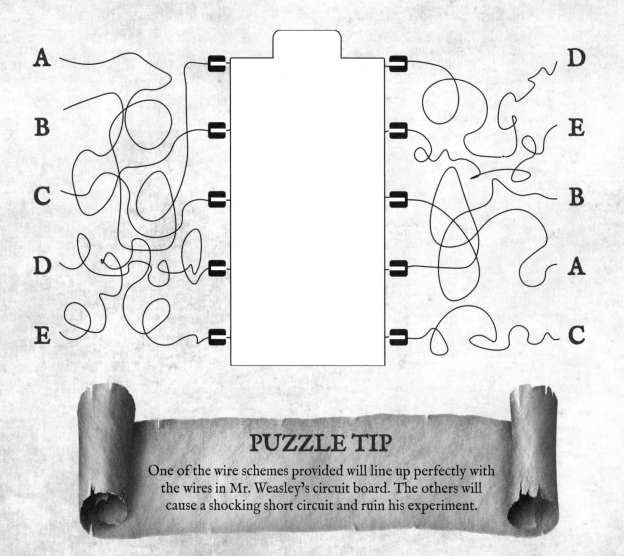

PUZZLE TIP

One of the wire schemes provided will line up perfectly with the wires in Mr. Weasley's circuit board. The others will cause a shocking short circuit and ruin his experiment.

Mr. Weasley leads the way to the Quidditch World Cup in *Harry Potter and the Goblet of Fire* (2005).

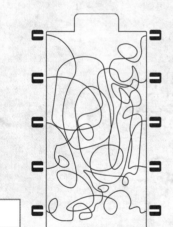

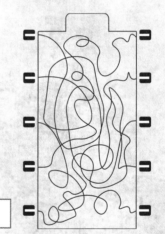

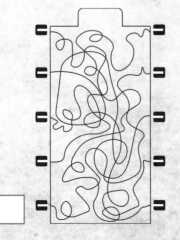

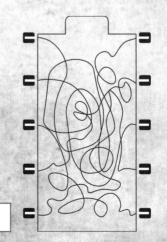

Magic Shadows

Can you tell which of the silhouettes opposite is a direct match?

Emma Watson as Hermione Granger.

Ho-Ho-Hogwarts

Why did Hermione bring her Time-Turner to the library?

TO BOOK MORE STUDY HOURS.

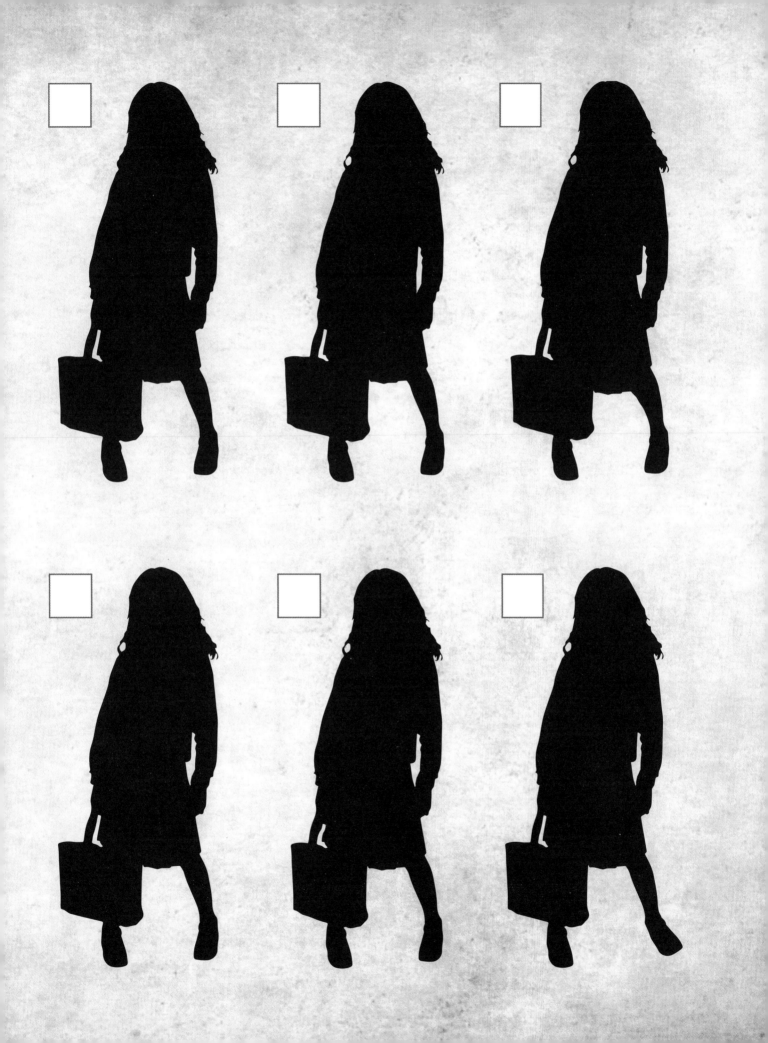

Hogwarts Curriculum

YEAR TWO

How closely were you paying attention to the *Harry Potter* books and films?

1. How many Ford Anglias were destroyed to film the scene in which Harry and Ron crash into the Whomping Willow?
  A. 14
  B. 10
  C. 4
  D. 7

2. Which special effect in the *CoS* film was practical rather than CGI?
  A. Tom Riddle's diary
  B. The door to the Chamber of Secrets
  C. The rogue bludger
  D. Dobby

3. There is a rumor that Dobby the house-elf's appearance in the films is based on this Russian politician:

_____ _____

4. Tom Felton improvised which line upon forgetting the correct one?
  A. "Scared, Potter?"
  B. "Training for the ballet, Potter?"
  C. "Famous Harry Potter can't even go into a bookshop without making the front page."
  D. "I didn't know you could read."

5. A perceptive viewer may notice this important item from *Half-Blood Prince* actually makes its first appearance in the Borgin and Burkes set in Knockturn Alley.

_____ _____

6. Who was originally cast as Gilderoy Lockhart but had to back out due to scheduling conflicts?
  A. Ewan McGregor
  B. Hugh Grant
  C. Christian Bale
  D. Jude Law

Rupert Grint as Ron Weasley in *Harry Potter and the Chamber of Secrets* (2002).

Miriam Margolyes as Professor Sprout in *Harry Potter and the Chamber of Secrets* (2002).

Hogwarts Curriculum
Continued

YEAR TWO

How closely were you paying attention to the *Harry Potter* books and films?

7. The faux title used to disguise the set by the crew was this Bruce Springsteen song:
   A. "Glory Days"
   B. "Tougher Than the Rest"
   C. "Incident on 57th Street"
   D. "Brilliant Disguise"

8. What are the seven ingredients of Polyjuice Potion?

_____

_____

_____

_____

_____

_____

9. This defensive charm, which causes an opponent to release whatever they are holding, was learned in the book's inaugural Dueling Club meeting.

_____

10. Hermione used this spell to freeze the pixies Lockhart unleashed on his second-year class in the book.

_____

11. In the book, Harry uses this spell on Malfoy to induce tickling during their duel.

_____

12. After Malfoy summons a snake in the book by shouting _____ during Dueling Club, Harry's Parseltongue abilities are revealed when he tells the snake to back off of Justin Finch-Fletchley.

Tom Felton as Draco Malfoy in *Harry Potter and the Chamber of Secrets* (2002).

Hogwarts Curriculum

Continued

YEAR TWO

How closely were you paying attention to the *Harry Potter* books and films?

13. In the book, Hermione uses _____ on Tom Riddle's diary in an attempt to reveal invisible ink. Unfortunately, this revealing charm does not work.

14. This spell was used by Snape to vanish the snake summoned by Malfoy during his duel with Harry in the book. _____ _____

15. This spell was used to blast away Acromantulas in order to save Ron and Harry from Aragog's children in the film.
_____ _____

16. _____ _____ is a counter-spell for general use and terminates all spell effects. It is used by Snape during a particularly chaotic Dueling Club practice in the book.

17. Can you fill in the blanks in Ginny's Valentine's poem to Harry?
"His eyes are as green as a fresh _____ _____,
His ____ is as dark as a blackboard.
I wish he was ____, he's truly divine,
the hero who conquered the ____ ____.""

18. Which of the following appeared at Nearly Headless Nick's Deathday Party in the book?
  A. Maggoty haggis
  B. Moldy cake
  C. Rotten deviled eggs
  D. Fungus-covered peanuts
  E. Chains for the ghosts to shake at their leisure
  F. A ghost orchestra featuring a musical saw
  G. Dull gray candles
  H. A grey cake shaped like a tombstone

Are You a Quidditch Expert?

If you can spot the fake Quidditch
rules, you're a star Seeker.

1. Chasers can pass the ball
between each other but only
one is allowed to enter into the
scoring zone at any one time.

REAL   FAKE

2. The winner of the
match is the team that
finds the Golden Snitch.

REAL   FAKE

3. Contact is allowed, but a
player may not seize hold of
another player's broomstick or
any part of their anatomy.

REAL   FAKE

4. There is no time limit to
a Quidditch game; it goes on
until the Snitch is found.

REAL   FAKE

5. During a penalty shot, though the Keeper maintains their position near the goals, any player may block an incoming shot on goal.

REAL   FAKE

6. If any member of the crowd casts a spell on a player, the benefitting team forfeits the game.

REAL   FAKE

7. If any player leaves the boundaries of the field, they surrender the Quaffle to the other team.

REAL   FAKE

8. Any player on the team may call time outs, which may be extended to two hours if a game has already lasted for more than 12 hours.

REAL   FAKE

BONUS During the Quidditch World Cup of 1473, every foul in the Quidditch rule book was committed. How many are there?

_____

Tom Felton as Draco Malfoy in *Harry Potter and the Chamber of Secrets* (2002).

Match Day Logic

Use logic to locate the Golden Snitch to help Harry defeat Slytherin on the pitch.

The Slytherin and Gryffindor teams in uniform for their match in *Harry Potter and the Chamber of Secrets* (2002).

IT'S GRYFFINDOR VS. SLYTHERIN, the most hotly contested Quidditch match of the year at Hogwarts. From their position on the field, Gryffindor's Seeker notices that the players and Quidditch balls in their view are arranged in a grid. What's more, they've just spotted the Snitch! Using the clues on the opposite page, can you fill in the blank grid and reveal its location?

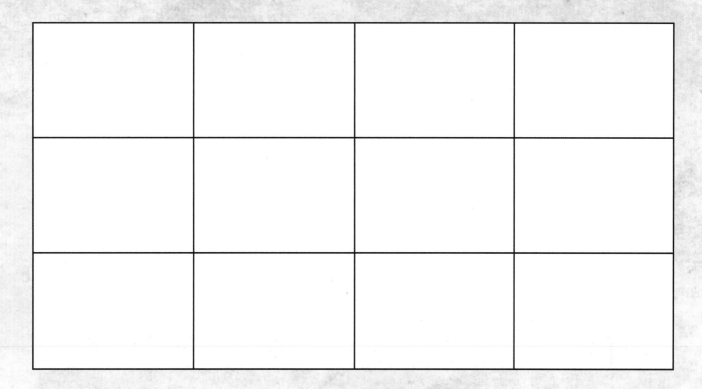

IN VIEW

Gryffindor Players

Katie Bell
Angelina Johnson
Alicia Spinnet
Fred Weasley
George Weasley

Slytherin Players

Marcus Flint
Draco Malfoy
Adrian Pucey

Quidditch Balls

Bludger #1
Bludger #2
Quaffle
Snitch

CLUES

1. Angelina Johnson is two spaces below Alicia Spinnet, who is two spaces to the left of Draco Malfoy, who is immediately above Bludger #2.

2. Fred Weasley is directly to the right of Bludger #1, which is two spaces below Adrian Pucey.

3. Adrian Pucey is two spaces to the right of George Weasley.

4. The Golden Snitch is below Marcus Flint, who is two spaces to the left of Katie Bell.

Enemies of the Heir, Beware

Can you match the five means of petrification to the six Hogwarts dwellers who met the gaze of the basilisk?

Daniel Radcliffe as Harry Potter in *Harry Potter and the Chamber of Secrets* (2002).

TCD/PROD.DB/ALAMY

A. Saw the basilisk's reflection in a hand mirror.

B. Saw the basilisk through a camera lens.

C. Saw the basilisk's reflection in a puddle caused by the flooding in the nearby bathroom.

D. Saw the basilisk through a ghost.

E. Looked the basilisk straight in the eye.

1. __ Mrs. Norris

2. __ Colin Creevey

3. __ Nearly Headless Nick

4. __ Justin Finch-Fletchley

5. __ Hermione Granger

6. __ Penelope Clearwater

Ha-Ha-Hogwarts
Did you hear about the special Transfiguration wand? IT CHANGES EVERYTHING.

Teacher of the Year

1. How many of his own books does Lockhart assign as textbooks for his class?
- A. 3
- B. 7
- C. 1
- D. 10

2. How many works did Lockhart publish in total? _____

3. How many times did Lockhart win *Witch Weekly*'s Most Charming Smile Award?
- A. 4
- B. 3
- C. 7
- D. 5

4. What is Lockhart's favorite color?
- A. Lilac
- B. Lavender
- C. Periwinkle
- D. Violet

5. Which house was Lockhart in as a student?

_____

6. Though Lockhart didn't actually take part in any of the feats detailed in his novels, at which charm was he most accomplished that helped him take credit for those deeds?
- A. Vanishing Spell
- B. Switching Spell
- C. Memory Charm
- D. Banishing Charm

7. Which spell does Lockhart use to try to immobilize the pixies he unleashes on his class?
- A. *Partis Temporus*
- B. *Peskipiksi Pesternomi*
- C. *Piertotum Locomotor*
- D. *Periculum*

8. How many points does Hermione earn for Gryffindor with a perfect score on Lockhart's biographical quiz?
- A. 5
- B. 100
- C. 10
- D. 20

9. Lockhart is an honorary member of which organization?
- A. Auror Office
- B. Dark Force Defense League
- C. Order of the Phoenix
- D. Order of Merlin

10. Which of the following is NOT a book by Gilderoy Lockhart?
- A. *Magical Me*
- B. *Playdate with a Poltergeist*
- C. *Holidays with Hags*
- D. *Wanderings with Werewolves*

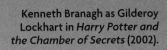

Professor Lockhart

Gilderoy in Print

Which are the real Gilderoy Lockhart titles hiding among the impostors?

Kenneth Branagh as Gilderoy Lockhart in *Harry Potter and the Chamber of Secrets* (2002).

WARNER BROS/PHOTOFEST

The Right Stuff

Can you follow the correct path to a successful Polyjuice Potion?

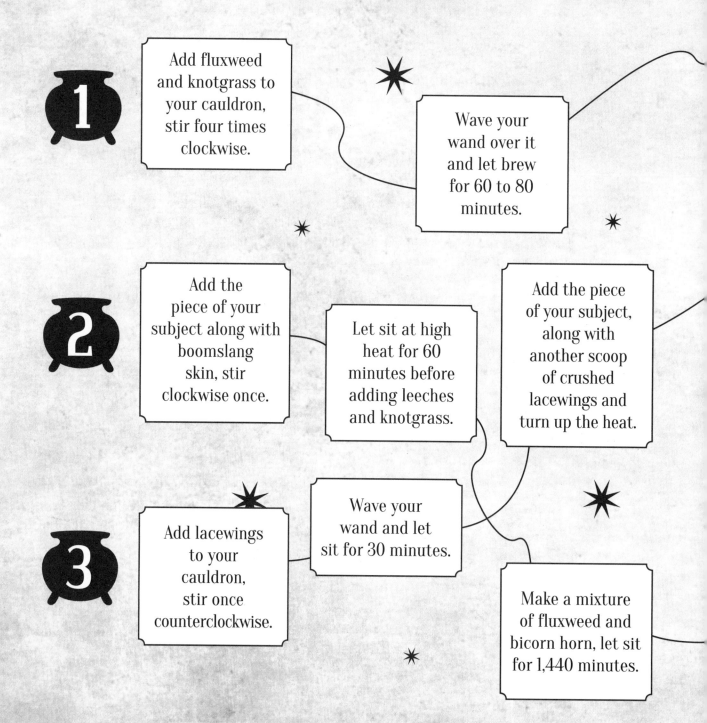

1 Add fluxweed and knotgrass to your cauldron, stir four times clockwise.

Wave your wand over it and let brew for 60 to 80 minutes.

2 Add the piece of your subject along with boomslang skin, stir clockwise once.

Let sit at high heat for 60 minutes before adding leeches and knotgrass.

Add the piece of your subject, along with another scoop of crushed lacewings and turn up the heat.

Wave your wand and let sit for 30 minutes.

3 Add lacewings to your cauldron, stir once counterclockwise.

Make a mixture of fluxweed and bicorn horn, let sit for 1,440 minutes.

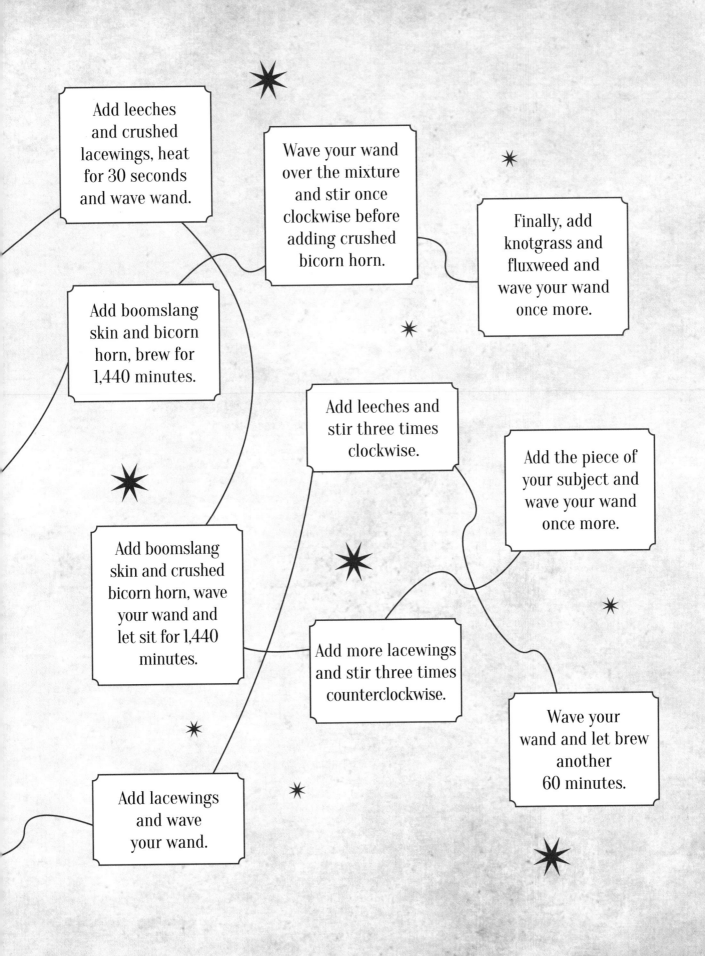

Add leeches and crushed lacewings, heat for 30 seconds and wave wand.

Wave your wand over the mixture and stir once clockwise before adding crushed bicorn horn.

Finally, add knotgrass and fluxweed and wave your wand once more.

Add boomslang skin and bicorn horn, brew for 1,440 minutes.

Add leeches and stir three times clockwise.

Add the piece of your subject and wave your wand once more.

Add boomslang skin and crushed bicorn horn, wave your wand and let sit for 1,440 minutes.

Add more lacewings and stir three times counterclockwise.

Wave your wand and let brew another 60 minutes.

Add lacewings and wave your wand.

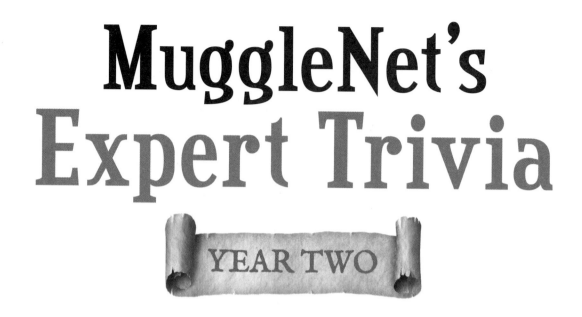

MuggleNet's
Expert Trivia

YEAR TWO

You must have been paying close attention to every
word of the saga if you can answer all of these questions.

1. Born to a Muggle father and witch mother,
this professor was the only one of his siblings
to display magical abilities.

_____

2. On a scale of X to XXXXX, what is the
Ministry of Magic classification for a Niffler?

_____

3. Caretaker Argus Filch claims there is a
list of how many forbidden items available
for perusal in his office?

_____

4. How many total chapters, including the
epilogue, are there in the *Harry Potter* series?

_____

5. Which charm will disable a
Muggle burglar alarm?

_____

6. Which charm did Gilderoy Lockhart
supposedly use to defeat the Wagga
Wagga Werewolf?

_____

7. Which charm does Ron use to remove
the lace from his Yule Ball dress robes?

_____

8. Who is Professor of Astronomy at Hogwarts?

_____

9. Who was famous for transfiguring
lost sailors into pigs?

_____

10. According to the Kwikspell pamphlet,
what animal form did D.J. Prod turn his
wife into as a testimonial?

_____

Owl post arrives at the Gryffindor table in *Harry Potter and the Chamber of Secrets* (2002).

Weasleys' Wizarding Clock

Determine which Weasley should go on each hand of the clock based on the description.

5. WORKS with dragons in Romania

4. WORKS at Gringotts in Egypt

3. ACCIDENTALLY places their arm in a butter dish at the Burrow

2. HAD their prefect badge bewitched to read "pinhead"

1. GETS in a fight with a Malfoy in Flourish and Blotts

6.CONSULTS a Gilderoy Lockhart book to complete a task at home

7.DRIVES the Flying Ford Anglia to save Harry from the Dursleys

8.RECEIVES a Howler in the Great Hall

9.PICKS the lock to the cupboard under the stairs to get Harry's Hogwarts supplies

James and Oliver Phelps as Fred and George, Rupert Grint as Ron and Bonnie Wright as Ginny.

YEAR THREE

HARRY POTTER

and the

PRISONER OF AZKABAN

As Harry returns to Hogwarts for his third year, a wanted
criminal is on the loose. But how dangerous is he really?

Alan Rickman as Severus Snape, Rupert Grint as Ron Weasley, Emma Watson as Hermione Granger and Daniel Radcliffe as Harry Potter in *Harry Potter and the Prisoner of Azkaban* (2004).

Ho-Ho-Hogwarts

Did you hear about the ghosts at Azkaban? THEY'RE DYING TO ESCAPE.

Gary Oldman as Sirius Black in *Harry Potter and the Prisoner of Azkaban* (2004).

Escape From Azkaban

Sirius Black is about to change into his Animagus form to sneak past the Dementors. Can you help him find his way out safely?

START

END

Hogwarts Curriculum

YEAR THREE

How closely were you paying attention to the *Harry Potter* books and films?

1. What assignment did Alfonso Cuarón give to Daniel Radcliffe, Rupert Grint and Emma Watson before filming began?
   A. Read *Prisoner of Azkaban*
   B. Write essays about their characters
   C. Both A and B

2. There's an Easter egg on the Marauder's Map the first time Harry opens it in the film. Whose name is shown?
   A. Newt Scamander
   B. Peter Pettigrew
   C. Richard Harris

3. What does Cuarón establish in the *Harry Potter* universe that will continue throughout the rest of the films?
   A. Modern-day, casual wardrobes for the students
   B. The castle's layout
   C. Both A and B

4. Who appears in the movie but has no lines?
   A. Parvati Patil
   B. Percy Weasley
   C. Dudley Dursley

5. In the film, the scene where Harry learns the Patronus Charm was originally going to take place in
   A. The Slytherin Common Room
   B. The Room of Requirement
   C. Dumbledore's office

Ho-Ho-Hogwarts

How did Hermione do on her third-year Charms final?

WAND-ERFULLY.

Emma Thompson as Sybill Trelawney in *Harry Potter and the Prisoner of Azkaban* (2004).

Hogwarts Curriculum

Continued

YEAR THREE

How closely were you paying attention to the *Harry Potter* books and films?

6. What are the names of the cats who portrayed Crookshanks in the film?
  A. Pumpkin and Crackerjack
  B. Fluffy and Ginger
  C. Muffin and Chester

7. When Harry arrives at the Leaky Cauldron in the film, a wizard is using magic to stir his mug. What Muggle book is he reading?

_____

8. The incantation _____ creates a dazzling light at the end of the wand, enabling the witch or wizard to see in the dark.

9. The charm _____ repels a boggart, but the word is not enough. _____ finishes it off.

10. In the movie, what spell does Hermione use to free Sirius from Dumbledore's office? _____

11. What doesn't the Patronus Charm project?
  A. Happiness
  B. Hope
  C. Despair
  D. The need to survive

12. When Peeves the Poltergeist blocks a keyhole with gum in the book, Professor Lupin teaches his class a spell, _____, that shoots the gum up Peeves's left nostril.
  A. *Mimblewimble*
  B. *Entomorphis*
  C. *Waddiwasi*
  D. *Terego*

13. In the book, Hermione uses _____ on Harry's glasses so he can see in the stormy conditions in the match against Hufflepuff.

Hogwarts Curriculum

Continued

YEAR THREE

How closely were you paying attention to the *Harry Potter* books and films?

14. What spell opens up hidden passageways?
  A. *Dissendium*
  B. *Alohomora*
  C. *Evanesco*
  D. *Obscuro*

15. During his Charms exam in the book, Harry accidentally overdoes the _____ Charm and causes Ron to laugh uncontrollably.

16. In the book, Dumbledore uses the incantation _____ _____ to stop Harry from smashing into the ground after falling off his broom.

17. What is the name of the password-protected secret passage that leads to Hogsmeade from Hogwarts?

_____

18. Ron finally bests the Whomping Willow years after the events of *Prisoner of Azkaban* using which charm?

_____

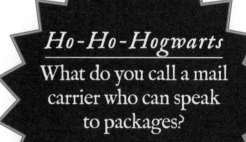

Ho-Ho-Hogwarts
What do you call a mail carrier who can speak to packages?
A PARCELMOUTH.

UNITED ARCHIVES GMBH/ALAMY

Jamie Waylett as Crabbe and Tom Felton as Draco Malfoy in *Harry Potter and the Prisoner of Azkaban* (2004).

Magic Shadows

Can you tell which of the silhouettes opposite is a direct match?

Rupert Grint as Ron Weasley.

WARNER BROS/EVERETT COLLECTION

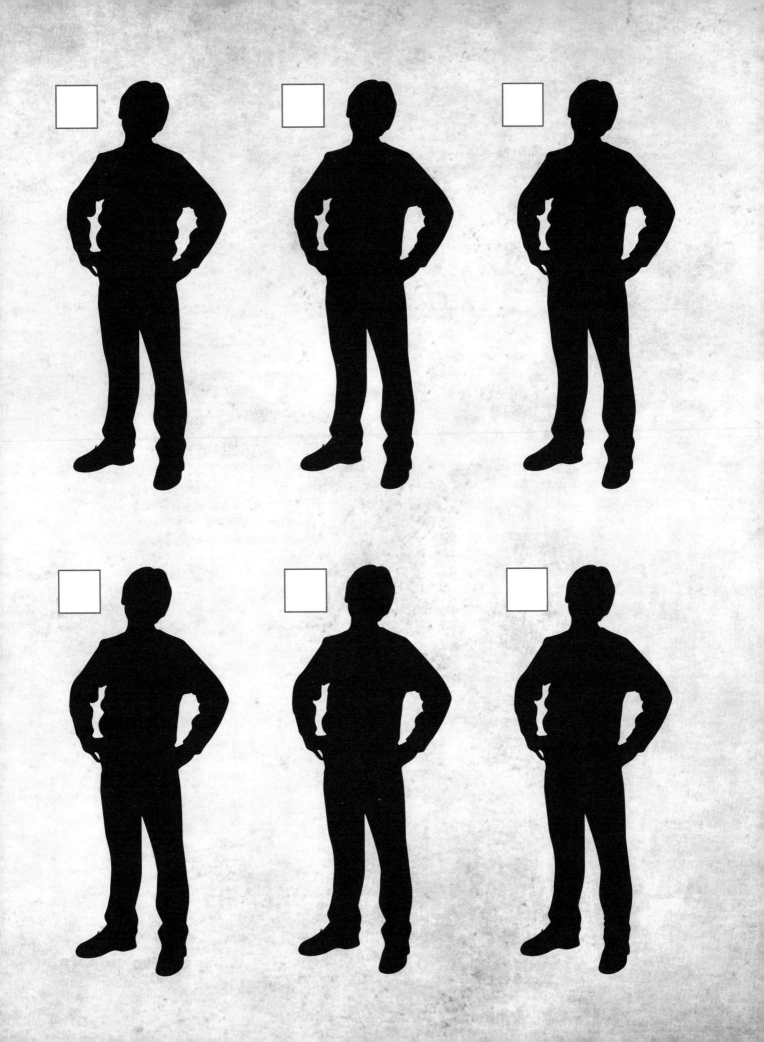

Teacher of the Year

1. What dark creatures do the third-years study in Lupin's class?
   A. Boggarts, Hinkypunks, Redcaps, Kappas, grindylows
   B. Boggarts, Hinkypunks, Redcaps, grindylows, werewolves
   C. Boggarts, Hinkypunks, Redcaps, grindylows, Dementors
   D. Boggarts, Hinkypunks, Redcaps, grindylows, vampires

2. When Snape takes over Lupin's class while he's ill, what page does Snape demand the class turn to?

_____

3. Who knows about Lupin's secret before he reunites with Sirius in the Shrieking Shack?
   A. Madam Pomfrey
   B. Hermione
   C. Malfoy
   D. A and B

4. Lupin's boggart turns into a _____ _____ when he faces it.

5. During his fifth year, Lupin's friends become _____ _____ so they can help him during the full moon.

6. Why does Sirius recommend Pettigrew as the Potters' Secret-Keeper instead of Lupin?
   A. Sirius didn't want to be it
   B. Sirius thought Lupin was the spy
   C. Lupin couldn't be a Secret-Keeper because he is a werewolf

7. Lupin forgets to say " _____ _____ " after spotting Pettigrew on the map, allowing _____ to use it.

8. What is Lupin's Patronus?

_____

9. What is Lupin's middle name?
   A. James
   B. Thomas
   C. John
   D. Bilius

10. In 2008, the British Independent Film Awards honored Lupin actor David Thewlis with an award named after which other *Harry Potter* actor?

_____

Professor Lupin

Hogsmeade Village

Can you unscramble the Hogsmeade landmarks
seen or visited by Harry and friends?

1. VESDIRH DAN ABGENS

_____

2. HTE O'HGS EHDA

_____

3. HNOEDKSUYE

_____

4. HSGEMOEDA TSATNOI

_____

5. ZKON'OS JEKO HSPO

_____

6. EHT HSRNIKEIG SAHKC

_____

7. TEH TEREH KOBROMSICST

_____

8. SHOMEGEDA TOSP FOFCIE

_____

9. MDAMA PDUDFOTIO'S TAE OHPS

_____

POST OFFICE ·OWL POST· POST OFFICE

·OWL POST·

POST OFFICE ·OWL POST·

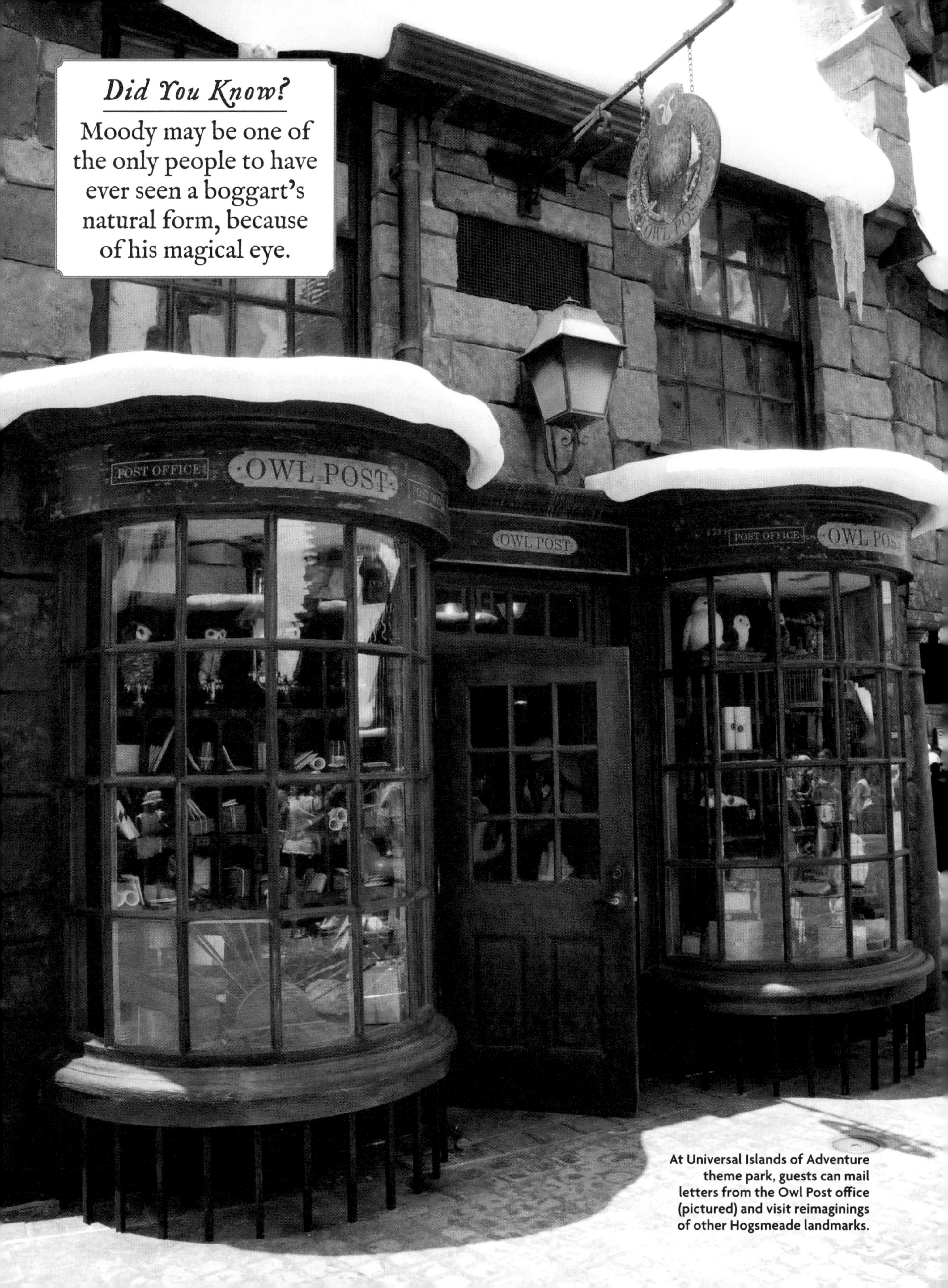

At Universal Islands of Adventure theme park, guests can mail letters from the Owl Post office (pictured) and visit reimaginings of other Hogsmeade landmarks.

Hagrid's Care of Magical Creatures Quiz

Do you remember Hagrid's first year of teaching well enough to pass his class?

Daniel Radcliffe as Harry Potter with Buckbeak – the hippogriff in *Harry Potter and the Prisoner of Azkaban* (2004).

ALBUM/ALAMY

1. Who was the Care of Magical Creatures professor before Hagrid?
  A. Professor Grubbly-Plank
  B. Professor Burbage
  C. Professor Kettleburn

2. Who helps Hagrid prepare Buckbeak's defense for the trial and appeal?
  A. Harry, Ron and Hermione
  B. Ron and Hermione
  C. Hermione

3. The book Hagrid assigns is called _____.

4. In the book, how many Hippogriffs does Hagrid show the class?
  A. 5
  B. 12
  C. 3

5. The class's Flobberworms die because they had too much _____.

6. Which student posits that future Care of Magical Creatures teacher Hagrid's large frame was the result of drinking too much Skele-Gro?
  A. Seamus Finnigan
  B. Lee Jordan
  C. Draco Malfoy
  D. Blaise Zabini

7. In a practical display of Care of Magical Creatures knowledge, which curse did Madame Maxime use against the giants to force them to drop Hagrid when they became violent later in the saga?
  A. Cruciatus
  B. Freezing
  C. Conjunctivitis
  D. Imperius

8. When did Hagrid begin teaching Care of Magical Creatures?
  A. December 1998
  B. September 1993
  C. September 1991
  D. December 1993

9. What is the first creature studied by Hagrid's Care of Magical Creatures class?
  A. Blast-Ended Skrewt
  B. Hippogriff
  C. Flobberworm
  D. Mandrake

10. Where did Hagrid claim to have had a slight disagreement with a vampire?
  A. Bratislava
  B. Vienna
  C. Minsk
  D. Ljubljana

Care of Magical Creatures

Harry and his classmates begin their studies of Care of Magical Creatures in third year. Can you unscramble each creature in their curriculum and match it to its description?

Robbie Coltrane as Hagrid, Emma Watson as Hermione Granger, Rupert Grint as Ron Weasley and Daniel Radcliffe as Harry Potter in *Harry Potter and the Prisoner of Azkaban* (2004).

WARNER BROS/PHOTOFEST

1. BSALT-NEEDD KSERTW

A fire-starting lizard, not to be confused with the non-magical animal of the same name.

_____

2. FHPOPIIRFG

An objectively boring herbivorous animal Draco Malfoy claims to have been bitten by.

_____

3. LOWBMERBORF

A creature created by Hagrid by cross-breeding Fire Crabs with manticores.

_____

4. SLADAMAREN

A creature with magical blood and a single horn on its forehead.

_____

5. INLFEFR

A horse-like creature invisible to those who have not witnessed death.

_____

6. TEHTRALS

An eagle-horse hybrid that proves essential to a _Prisoner of Azkaban_ escape plan.

_____

7. NUCORIN

A creature obsessed with shiny objects that becomes a main character in the _Fantastic Beasts_ films.

_____

The Monster Book of Monsters as it appears in *Harry Potter and the Prisoner of Azkaban* (2004).

Monster Book of Word Jumbles

Can you unscramble the animals that can be found in the infamous Care of Magical Creatures textbook?

HAGRID'S ADDITION to the Care of Magical Creatures curriculum, *The Monster Book of Monsters*, has a habit of shredding anything in its path if it's not soothed with a tickle on the spine. That, unfortunately, includes one unlucky student's notes. They've been torn to shreds! Can you put the pieces back together in order, revealing the relevant magical beasts?

1. X O D Y

2. P A P K A

3. U N N U D

4. A W C I D L I R

5. G R A T G O B

6. W U C K B O L E R T

7. R O E W O P F

8. I M E G S E D U I

9. P O G H A R N R

The Jinxed Gobstone

The Hogwarts Gobstones Club has been pranked! Can you help them discover which of their marbles has been jinxed?

SOMEONE HAS PLAYED a prank on the oft-maligned Hogwarts Gobstones Club, filling one of their stones with a potent new acne-inflamer from Weasleys' Wizard Wheezes that'll give them a barbershop quartet of huge singing forehead pimples. The good news is that the contaminated marble weighs a scant half a gram more than the normal ones. Snape has lent them a two-pan scale from his supplies but will only allow them to make two measurements before he takes it back. He claims that's more than enough to figure out which marble is contaminated. How can you use the scale in two measurements to determine which of the eight Gobstones in the bag has been jinxed? Remember, you only have two weighings to narrow it down.

Oliver and James Phelps as the Weasley twins.

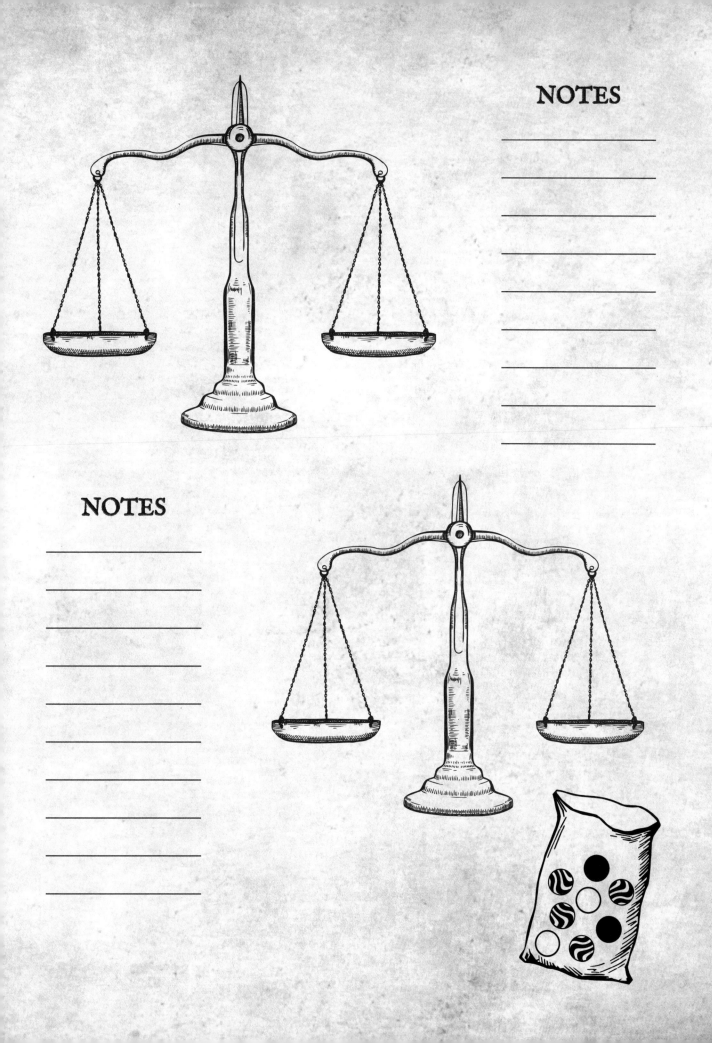

NOTES

_____

_____

_____

_____

_____

_____

_____

_____

_____

NOTES

_____

_____

_____

_____

_____

_____

_____

_____

Hermione's Impossible Schedule

Can you name the subjects in Hermione's schedule, so packed it requires the manipulation of time and space?

Emma Watson as Hermione Granger and Daniel Radcliffe as Harry Potter in *Harry Potter and the Prisoner of Azkaban* (2004).

PICTURELUX/THE HOLLYWOOD ARCHIVE/ALAMY

1. _____, Professor Snape

2. _____, Professor Lupin

3. _____, Hagrid

4. _____, Professor Vector

5. _____, Professor Trelawney

6. _____, Professor Burbage

7. _____, Professor Sprout

8. _____, Professor McGonagall

9. _____, Professor Flitwick

10. _____,
Professor Babbling

11. _____,
Professor Binns

12. _____,
Professor Sinistra

The Eye of the Seer

Professor Sybill Trelawney introduces Harry and his fellow third years to the imprecise art of Divination. Test your memory and determine whether these statements are true or false.

1. Trelawney predicts Neville would break his teacup on the first day of Divination.

2. *Harry Potter and the Prisoner of Azkaban* is the only book in the series in which Voldemort does not appear.

3. Trelawney warns the class one of their number would leave them forever around June.

4. During Christmas dinner, Trelawney says the first person to leave the table of 13 will die, and she ends up being correct.

5. When Trelawney finally makes a true prediction about Voldemort reuniting with his servant, she doesn't believe it to be true.

6. Trelawney's classroom is located in the North Tower on the seventh floor.

7. She sees the Grim in Harry's tea leaves and the crystal ball.

Ho-Ho-Hogwarts

What's it called when a wizard is robbed by a non-magical person? GETTING MUG-GLED.

Emma Thompson as Sybill Trelawney in *Harry Potter and the Prisoner of Azkaban* (2004).

MuggleNet's Expert Trivia

YEAR THREE

You must have been paying close attention to every word of the saga if you can answer all of these questions.

Maggie Smith as Minerva McGonagall in *Harry Potter and the Prisoner of Azkaban* (2004).

1. What is Harry's room number in Diagon Alley when he stays prior to starting his third year at Hogwarts?

_____

2. How many beds are on each level of the Knight Bus?

_____

3. What is the difference between male and female Blast-Ended Skrewts?

_____

4. Who was McGonagall's first love?

_____

5. What is the punishment for performing one of the Unforgivable Curses?
  A. Death
  B. A 1,000,000-Galleon fine
  C. Life in Azkaban
  D. 10 years in Azkaban unless it's performed on a Muggle

6. What is the purpose of burning sage and Mallowsweet and looking for various shapes and symbols in the fumes?

_____

7. On the first day of Divination, who does Professor Trelawney say should beware a redheaded man?
  A. Hermione Granger
  B. Luna Lovegood
  C. Padma Patil
  D. Parvati Patil

8. On which date does Trelawney predict the thing that Lavender Brown was dreading would happen?
  A. October 16
  B. February 1
  C. July 3
  D. September 19

9. Which relative of Trelawney's was a famous Seer?
  A. Her aunt
  B. Her cousin
  C. Her mother
  D. Her great-great-grandmother

10. Who is the only member of the trio to take Muggle Studies?

_____

The Marauder's Map

After solemnly swearing one is up to no good, Hogwarts and the surrounding environs become easier to navigate than Hogsmeade's high street. Can you fill in the blanks, revealing the castle's secret connections?

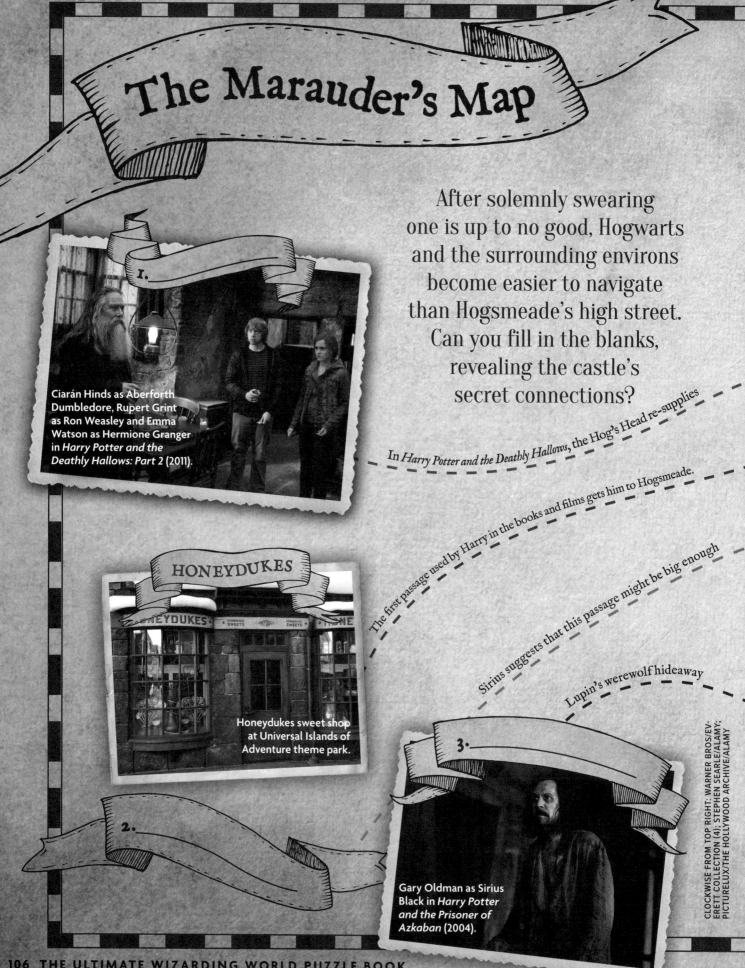

1. Ciarán Hinds as Aberforth Dumbledore, Rupert Grint as Ron Weasley and Emma Watson as Hermione Granger in *Harry Potter and the Deathly Hallows: Part 2* (2011).

HONEYDUKES

Honeydukes sweet shop at Universal Islands of Adventure theme park.

In *Harry Potter and the Deathly Hallows*, the Hog's Head re-supplies

The first passage used by Harry in the books and films gets him to Hogsmeade.

Sirius suggests that this passage might be big enough

Lupin's werewolf hideaway

2.

3.

Gary Oldman as Sirius Black in *Harry Potter and the Prisoner of Azkaban* (2004).

BORGIN AND BURKES

5.

Twin Vanishing Cabinets

One-eyed witch statue outside the Defense Against the Dark Arts classroom

Dumbledore's Army:

Gregory the Smarmy statue

Fred and George's first find is never explained further.

Mirror on the fourth floor

Tom Felton as Draco Malfoy in *Harry Potter and the Half-Blood Prince* (2009).

4.

to hold meetings in *Harry Potter and the Order of the Phoenix,* but it is caved in.

Hogwarts Castle and the Whomping Willow as seen in *Harry Potter and the Prisoner of Azkaban* (2004).

WHOMPING WILLOW

?

David Bradley as Argus Filch in *Harry Potter and the Prisoner of Azkaban* (2004).

✳ ARGUS FILCH'S ✳ SECRET PASSAGES

When Fred and George give Harry the map, they specify three passages that are still intact but unfortunately known to Argus Filch, the caretaker, which means his feline spy, Mrs. Norris, could be lurking in any of them waiting to catch a student out of line.

HARRY POTTER

and the

GOBLET OF FIRE

Harry's fourth year at Hogwarts is also the
year the wizarding world changes forever.

Michael Gambon as Albus Dumbledore in *Harry Potter and the Goblet of Fire* (2005).

Diagon Alley Mix-Up

Can you fix the magically mixed-up image?

A MISCHIEVOUS POLTERGEIST fond of haunting the *Daily Prophet*'s offices has magically split this image of Diagon Alley into pieces and rotated or flipped 12 of them. Can you pick out which ones have been altered (and how) to help fix the image?

The Quidditch World Cup

How well do you recall the match?

1. What's the name of the magical binoculars Harry buys for himself, Ron and Hermione?
A. Omnioculars
B. Unioculars
C. Owloculars

2. Ludo Bagman is the head of _____.
A. Magical Law Enforcement
B. Magical Games and Sports
C. International Magical Cooperation

3. Which one of these players is not on the Bulgarian team?
A. Vulchanov
B. Zograf
C. Dragomir

4. How much money do the Weasley twins bet Bagman that Ireland will win, but Bulgaria will catch the snitch?
A. 35 Gallons, 15 Sickles and 3 Knuts
B. 37 Gallons, 15 Sickles and 3 Knuts
C. 37 Gallons, 15 Sickles and 4 Knuts

5. Which one of these players is not on the Ireland team?
A. Quigley
B. Murphy
C. Mullet

6. Why is Barty Crouch Sr.'s absence so notable?
A. His elf, Winky, is saving a seat for him
B. Fudge expected Crouch to help with the Bulgarian Minister
C. Both A and B

7. Viktor Krum's signature move, which he uses against Irish Seeker Lynch, is the _____ _____.

8. Mr. Weasley advises the boys to _____ _____ _____ to avoid becoming entranced by the Veela.

9. The final score of the World Cup is Ireland _____, Bulgaria ____.

Did You Know?

After Harry sends the food package to Sirius, he sees an eagle owl with a note in its beak soar past Hagrid's hut toward the castle. That eagle owl is carrying Voldemort's order to Barty Crouch Jr. that he should stop Barty Crouch Sr., who had escaped, at all costs.

Exhibited memorabilia from the Quidditch storyline in *Harry Potter and the Goblet of Fire* (2005).

The Championship Teams

The rosters of the Irish and Bulgarian national Quidditch teams are listed to the right. Can you spot the three fake names on each team?

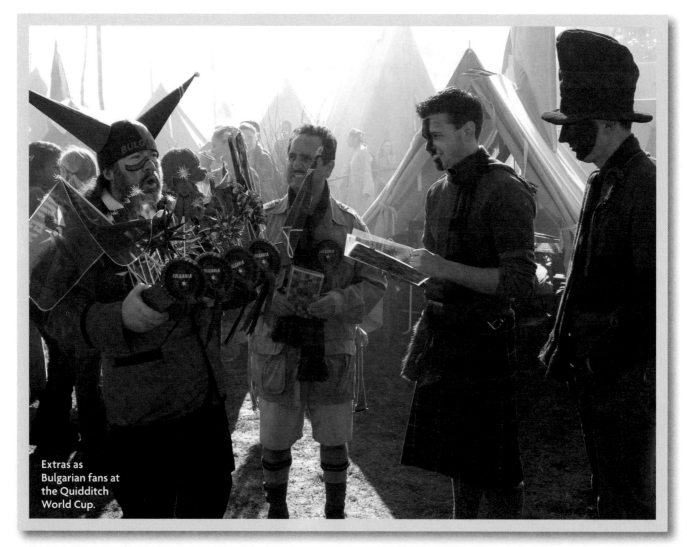

Extras as Bulgarian fans at the Quidditch World Cup.

IRELAND

MULLET

MORAN

TROY

McGILLICUDDY

O'HARA

CONNOLLY

RYAN

QUIGLEY

LYNCH

O'BRIAN

BULGARIA

DIMITROV

IVANOVA

ZHUKOV

KORNOVA

LEVSKI

VULCHANOV

VOLKOV

KRUM

ZOGRAF

NABOKOV

Professional Teams of
Britain and Ireland

Can you prove your seeking skills and match the locations with their pro Quidditch team's name?

Kestrels   Falcons   Arrows

Wasps   Pride   Catapults

Cannons   Magpies   Tornadoes

United   Harpies

Wanderers   Bats

1. Ballycastle _____   **8.** Caerphilly _____

2. Puddlemere _____   **9.** Holyhead _____

3. Montrose _____   **10.** Wimbourne _____

4. Kenmare _____   **11.** Chudley _____

5. Tutshill _____   **12.** Wigtown _____

6. ____ of Portree   **13.** Falmouth _____

7. Appleby _____

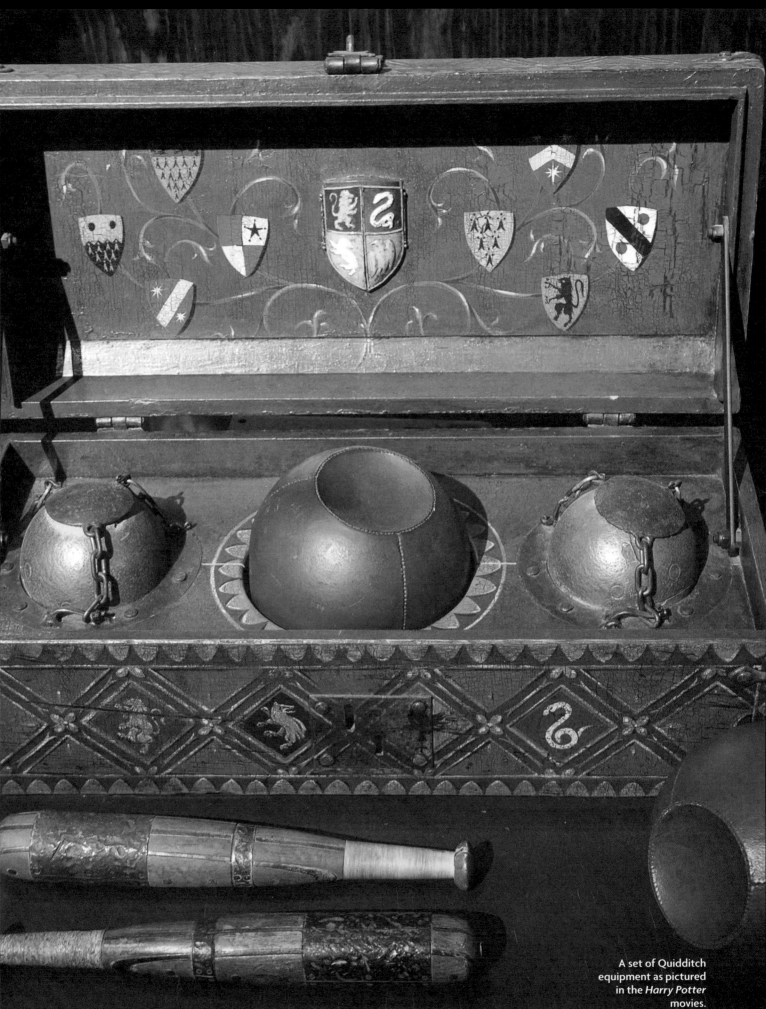

A set of Quidditch equipment as pictured in the *Harry Potter* movies.

Hogwarts Curriculum

YEAR FOUR

How closely were you paying attention to the *Harry Potter* books and films?

1. Daniel Radcliffe's costars got to practice the Yule Ball dance routine for three weeks. How much time did he get?
 A. Four days
 B. Four months
 C. One week

2. Members of which English bands made up the Weird Sisters in the film?
 A. The Rolling Stones and Led Zeppelin
 B. Pulp and Radiohead
 C. Pulp and Blur

Ho-Ho-Hogwarts:
What do you call someone from Slytherin House who is really into French pastry?
DRACO MILLE-FEUILLE.

3. Which of these characters appeared in the movie?
 A. Winky
 B. Ludo Bagman
 C. Walden Macnair

4. During the film's graveyard scene, the names of Voldemort's paternal grandparents are revealed, though they are never mentioned in the book. What are they?
 A. Thomas Riddle Sr. and Patricia Riddle
 B. Thomas Riddle Sr. and Jane Riddle
 C. Thomas Riddle Sr. and Mary Riddle

5. *The Goblet of Fire* is the first film in the franchise to
 A. Not feature Molly Weasley
 B. Star Richard Harris as Dumbledore
 C. Be directed by David Yates

WARNER BROS/EVERETT COLLECTION

Rupert Grint as Ron Weasley, Alfred Enoch as Dean Thomas, Matthew Lewis as Neville Longbottom and Daniel Radcliffe as Harry Potter in *Harry Potter and the Goblet of Fire* (2005).

Hogwarts Curriculum

Continued

YEAR FOUR

How closely were you paying attention to the *Harry Potter* books and films?

6. How much time did Daniel Radcliffe have to spend underwater shooting the second task? _____

7. In the book, Harry uses the incantation _____, which he learned in Flitwick's Charms class, to summon his Firebolt in the first task.

8. The _____ _____ is the opposite of the Summoning Charm.

9. Used most frequently in the books by Ludo Bagman, _____ is a charm that amplifies the caster's voice.

10. _____ is an incantation Death Eaters use to conjure the Dark Mark.

David Tennant as Barty Crouch Jr. in *Harry Potter and the Goblet of Fire* (2005).

Hogwarts Curriculum

Continued

YEAR FOUR

How closely were you paying attention to the *Harry Potter* books and films?

11. The incantation _____ is often used in combat and renders the target semi- or unconscious.

12. The _____ Curse blasts obstacles apart.

13. Both Fleur and Cedric use the _____ - _____ Charm in the second task, which allowed them to survive underwater.

14. In the book, Harry used the incantation _____ to slow down Hagrid's Blast-Ended Skrewt in the maze.

15. The _____ Spell causes the caster's wand to turn into a compass and point north.

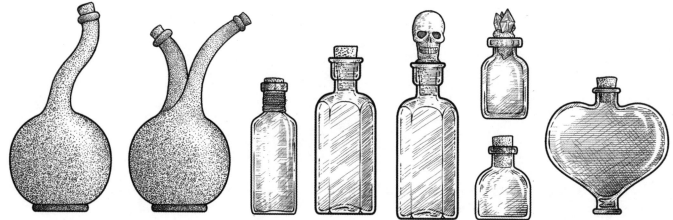

Angelica Mandy as Gabrielle Delacour and Clémence Poésy as Fleur Delacour in *Harry Potter and the Goblet of Fire* (2005).

The World of
Wizarding Schools

Though Harry Potter's story takes place largely at Hogwarts, there are wizarding stories taking place at schools all over the world. Can you fill in the names of the schools?

Did You Know?

Natalie McDonald, a first-year Sorted into Gryffindor, is named after a real girl who died of leukemia.

1. A golden edifice in the Brazilian rainforest that appears to be a ruin to Muggles, just like Hogwarts.

_____

3. Located on an "uninhabited" volcanic island, this school begins accepting students at age 7.

_____

2. Though smaller wizarding schools exist throughout Africa, this school draws students from every country on the continent. It is the largest wizarding school in the world.

_____

4. The North American wizarding school, modeled after Hogwarts, can be found at Mount Greylock in Massachusetts.

_____

③

5. Hidden in the Scottish Highlands is this school, which serves as the main setting for the _Harry Potter_ saga and is the first one to be set on paper by J.K. Rowling.

_____

6. It is largely Gellert Grindelwald's attendance that gives this northern European institution its dark reputation.

_____

7. The French wizarding academy can be found somewhere in the Pyrenees Mountains and is also the alma mater of Nicolas Flamel.

_____

The Yule Ball

Can you match the characters with their dates to the dance?

1. __ Harry Potter
2. __ Ron Weasley
3. __ Hermione Granger
4. __ Cedric Diggory
5. __ Ginny Weasley
6. __ Fleur Delacour
7. __ Seamus Finnigan
8. __ Fred Weasley

A. Neville Longbottom
B. Angelina Johnson
C. Parvati Patil
D. Roger Davies
E. Viktor Krum
F. Padma Patil
G. Lavender Brown
H. Cho Chang

Alan Rickman as Severus Snape, Maggie Smith as Minerva McGonagall and Michael Gambon as Albus Dumbledore in *Harry Potter and the Goblet of Fire* (2005).

FROM LEFT: WARNER BROS/EVERETT COLLECTION; TCD/PROD.DB/ALAMY

Daniel Radcliffe as Harry Potter and Rupert Grint as Ron Weasley in *Harry Potter and the Goblet of Fire* (2005).

Teacher of the Year

1. What can Moody's magical eye see through?
  A. Invisibility cloaks
  B. Solid objects
  C. Both A and B

2. What does Professor McGonagall reprimand Moody for?
  A. Casting Unforgivable Curses on students
  B. Using Transfiguration as punishment
  C. Helping Harry with the second task

3. How does Barty Crouch Jr. break free after his father puts him under house arrest?
  A. Polyjuice Potion
  B. Peter Pettigrew and Voldemort find him
  C. He is an unregistered Animagus

4. Disguised as Mad-Eye, Barty Crouch Jr. suggests that Harry become a(n) _____ after Hogwarts.

5. When does Dumbledore realize Professor Moody is an impostor?
  A. After he asks to take the Cup into the maze
  B. After he takes Harry back to the castle
  C. When the Polyjuice Potion wears off

6. Mad-Eye Moody lost a chunk of his nose fighting the Death Eater _____.

7. The real Moody is revealed to be hidden in his own _____ and under the _____ Curse.

8. While practicing hex-deflection in Defense Against the Dark Arts class with Moody, which hex is Harry hit with?
  A. Bat Bogey Hex
  B. Cruciatus Curse
  C. Twitchy Ears Hex
  D. Hurling Hex

Ho-Ho-Hogwarts:
What do you call Quidditch players who share a dormitory?
BROOM-MATES.

ALBUM/ALAMY

Professor Moody

The Triwizard Tournament

Facing dragons, grindylows and sphinxes, the four champions are up against dangerous obstacles. See how well you remember the Tournament.

THE FIRST TASK

1. On which date does the first task take place?
  A. October 31
  B. November 16
  C. November 24

2. Cedric turns a _____ into a _____ to try to get his dragon to go for it instead.

3. What score does Karkaroff give Harry?
  A. 1
  B. 3
  C. 4

THE SECOND TASK

1. In the book, who gives Harry the Gillyweed minutes before the second task?
  A. Neville
  B. Dobby
  C. Moody

2. Harry earns _____ points in the second task, tying with _____ _____.

3. Harry brings _____ _____ and _____ _____up from the lake.

THE THIRD TASK

1. What's the first obstacle Harry encounters in the maze?
  A. The Sphinx
  B. Blast-Ended Skrewt
  C. Boggart

2. The answer to the Sphinx's riddle is " _____."

3. As Harry and Cedric both grab the Triwizard Cup, they realize it's a _____.

Daniel Radcliffe as Harry Potter in *Harry Potter and the Goblet of Fire* (2005).

The Triwizard Maze

Can you find your way to the center of the maze before the other Triwizard champions?

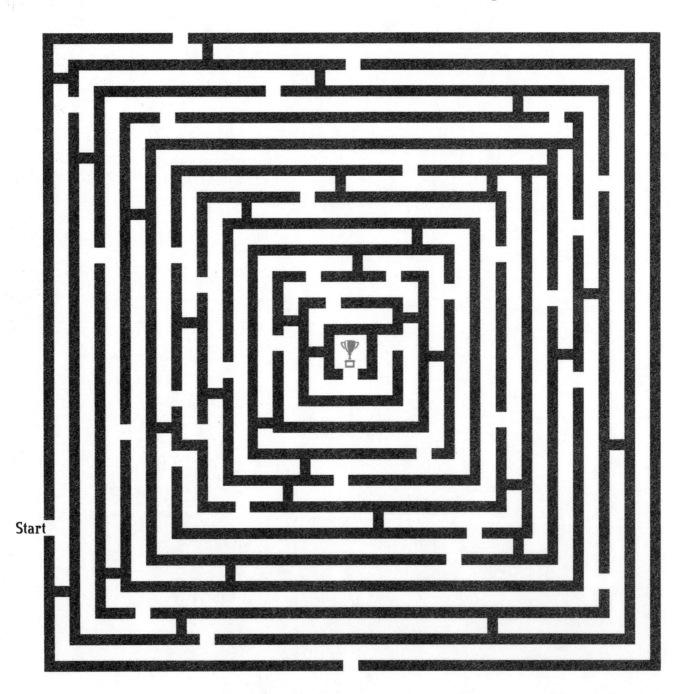

Start

Robert Pattinson as Cedric Diggory in *Harry Potter and the Goblet of Fire* (2005).

Voldemort Returns

See how well you remember
that fateful night in the graveyard.

1. The ingredients of Voldemort's
resurrection are:
  A. Bone of the father, willingly given;
      flesh of the servant, unwillingly given;
      and blood of the enemy, forcibly taken.
  B. Bone of the father, forcibly taken;
      flesh of the servant, willingly given; and
      blood of the enemy, willingly given
  C. Bone of the father, unknowingly given;
      flesh of the servant, willingly given; and
      blood of the enemy, forcibly taken

2. What color does the potion turn
after all the ingredients and Voldemort
are added?
  A. Red   B. Green   C. White

3. Peter Pettigrew helps Voldemort return
to a rudimentary body in the beginning
of *Goblet of Fire* with a few spells, a couple
of unspeakable acts and a potion of _____
blood and ____ venom from _____.

4. Harry throws off the _____ ____
and refuses to _____ to Voldemort
before their duel.

5. Which Death Eater(s) miss Voldemort's
rebirthing party?
  A. Nott
  B. The Lestranges
  C. Crabbe Sr. and Goyle Sr.

6. Who unwittingly helps Voldemort
reunite with his most faithful servant?
  A. Frank Bryce
  B. Barty Crouch Jr.
  C. Bertha Jorkins

7. When Harry makes his last stand against
Voldemort, he meets the Killing Curse with
the incantation _____.

8. Who is the fourth person to
appear out of Voldemort's wand
during *Priori Incantatem*?
  A. Lily Potter
  B. James Potter
  C. Bertha Jorkins

9. On what date does Voldemort return?
_____

10. Which word does Voldemort use to
describe Cedric Diggory just before
Wormtail kills him?
  A. Extra
  B. Other
  C. Spare
  D. Bonus

Ralph Fiennes as Lord Voldemort in *Harry Potter and the Goblet of Fire* (2005).

Michael Gambon as
Albus Dumbledore in
*Harry Potter and the
Goblet of Fire* (2005).

MuggleNet's Expert Trivia

YEAR FOUR

You must have been paying close attention to every word of the saga if you can answer all of these questions.

1. Bathilda Bagshot sends an owl to Dumbledore after being impressed by his article on what topic in *Transfiguration Today?*

_____

2. Name this professor's wand: 10 1/4, cypress tree, unicorn hair, pliable.

_____

3. With the front half of a horse and the back end of the fish, this creature shares a name with a part of the human brain.

_____

4. Herpo the Foul created the first what?

_____

5. What type of wand wood has a reputation for performing best for Seers and those skilled in Legilimency?

_____

6. Who was the first Supreme Mugwump of the International Confederation of Wizards?

_____

7. What famous witch first discovered the magical properties of Gillyweed?

_____

8. The Triwizard Tournament was first established in what year?

_____

9. Who invented the Sneakoscope?

_____

10. In what year was the Department of Magical Games and Sports established at the Ministry of Magic?

_____

YEAR FIVE

HARRY POTTER
and the
ORDER OF THE PHOENIX

Voldemort is back, but the wizarding world refuses
to believe it, as Harry prepares for his O.W.L.s.

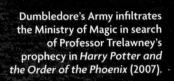

Dumbledore's Army infiltrates the Ministry of Magic in search of Professor Trelawney's prophecy in *Harry Potter and the Order of the Phoenix* (2007).

Lost in Muggle London

Can you help an absent-minded Muggle Studies
student find his way to the Portkey home?

THE N.E.W.T.-LEVEL MUGGLE STUDIES students at Hogwarts have been assigned a bit of fieldwork over their holiday break: visiting the British Museum for the day and submitting two scrolls of parchment on an artifact of their choosing. One particularly absent-minded member of the class has been so caught up in exploring the museum he's lost track of time and is about to miss the Portkey that will take him back to Godric's Hollow, where he's spending the holiday with friends. He's not quite sure where the Portkey is, but he's just noticed another student from his group rushing out the door. Using the map of London provided, can you follow in their footsteps and reveal the location of the Portkey home?

THE STUDENT...

Exits the British Museum onto Great Russell Street.

Makes a right onto Southampton Row.

Makes a right onto Hart Street.

Follows Hart Street to Drury Lane and makes a left.

Makes a right onto Russell Street and follows it to the London landmark where you'll find the Portkey.

What is the landmark?

_____

Your O.W.L. Exams

YEAR FIVE

Use your comprehensive knowledge from the past five years at Hogwarts to see if you can master this expert-level grab bag of wizarding knowledge.

1. A _____ _____ is used to swap two different objects for one another.
  A. Swapping Spell
  B. Switching Spell
  C. Switch Charm
  D. Trading Spell

2. What is the result of the incantation *Flintifors?*
  A. Turns a desk into a pig
  B. Turns a rabbit into a slipper
  C. Turns the target into a matchbox
  D. Turns the target into a snuffbox

3. The incantation _____ _____ transforms an animal into a goblet.
  A. *Vera Verto*
  B. *Ventus Duo*
  C. *Verdimillious Duo*
  D. *Vulnera Sanentur*

4. Holding a mandrake leaf in one's mouth for a month and reciting a specific incantation on a daily basis is part of the process of:
  A. Becoming an Animagus
  B. Keeping your human mind during werewolf transformations
  C. Becoming a Metamorphmagus
  D. Permanently changing your hair color

5. What is the incantation for the Bird-Conjuring Charm?
  A. *Avifors*   B. *Anteoculatia*
  C. *Anapneo*   D. *Avis*

6. The incantation *Evanesco*:
  A. Causes the target to grow in size
  B. Transforms the target into an insectoid for a short time
  C. Vanishes both animate and inanimate objects
  D. Adheres one object to another

WARNER BROS/EVERETT COLLECTION

Hogwarts students sit for their exams in the Great Hall, rearranged from its usual four-table setup.

Your O.W.L. Exams
Continued

YEAR FIVE

Use your comprehensive knowledge from the past five years at Hogwarts to see if you can master this expert-level grab bag of wizarding knowledge.

7. Monkshood and wolfsbane are also known as:
  A. Wormwood
  B. Aconite
  C. Asphodel
  D. Moondew

8. Approximately how long does it take to brew a Polyjuice Potion?
  A. Three months
  B. Two weeks
  C. One month
  D. Two months

9. A _____ _____ is used to soothe a person after experiencing shock, trauma or an emotional outburst.
  A. Soothing Solution
  B. Calming Draught
  C. Draught of Peace
  D. Girding Potion

10. Who replaces Trelawney after Umbridge fires her during Harry's fifth year?
  A. Bane
  B. Firenze
  C. Ronan
  D. Magorian

11. Name the four lessons Snape taught his students in Year 5 (that we know of):
  (1) _____
  (2) _____
  (3) _____
  (4) _____

12. Which potion does Snape brew for Lupin during Harry's third year?
  A. Wolfsbane Potion
  B. Wormwood Potion
  C. Wiggenweld Potion
  D. Strengthening Solution

13. Name each DA member's Patronus:
Harry Potter _____
Ron Weasley _____
Hermione Granger _____
Ginny Weasley _____
Cho Chang _____
Luna Lovegood _____
Seamus Finnigan _____
Ernie Macmillan _____

Hogwarts students amass in the courtyard.

Your O.W.L. Exams

Continued

YEAR FIVE

Use your comprehensive knowledge from the past five years at Hogwarts to see if you can master this expert-level grab bag of wizarding knowledge.

14. List the incantation for all three Unforgivable Curses:

The Killing Curse _____

The Imperius Curse _____

The Cruciatus Curse _____

15. Which of the following is NOT a defensive spell?

  A. *Stupefy*   B. *Impedimenta*
  C. *Expecto Patronum*   D. *Incendio*

16. Which of the following is the incantation for the Shield Charm?

  A. *Protego*   B. *Protecto*
  C. *Portus*   D. *Petrificus Totalus*

17. Trelawney's great-great-grandmother was a famous Seer.
What was her name?

  A. Caroline   B. Cassie
  C. Cassandra   D. Carolyn

18. Complete the prophecy (one point per answer): "Neither can _____ while the other _____."

19. How many legitimate prophecies has Trelawney made (that we know of)?

  A. 3   B. 2   C. 1   D. 5

20. Which of the following studies of Divination was NOT taught in Trelawney's class?

  A. Dream interpretation
  B. Crystal ball reading
  C. Tea leaf reading
  D. Bone reading

21. Which room in the Department of Mysteries contains all records of prophecies made?

  A. The Hall of Prophecies
  B. The Future Foyer
  C. The Department of the Divine
  D. The Room of Prophecies

22. What is the best incantation to use against a boggart?

  A. *Ridiculous*   B. *Riddikulus*
  C. *Ridonkulous*   D. *Ridiklis*

Bonnie Wright as Ginny Weasley and Oliver and James Phelps as her brothers Fred and George in *Harry Potter and the Order of the Phoenix* (2007).

Your O.W.L. Exams
Continued

YEAR FIVE

Use your comprehensive knowledge from the past five years at Hogwarts to see if you can master this expert-level grab bag of wizarding knowledge.

23. Can you put these events in the proper order using the letters A through L?

____ Padfoot has his last laugh.

____ Order of the Phoenix members rescue Harry from the Dursleys and take him to Sirius's childhood home.

____ Mr. Weasley is attacked by Voldemort's snake while on Order of the Phoenix duty.

____ Harry receives his first detention from Umbridge and learns the cost of telling "lies."

____ Hagrid shows Harry and Hermione what he's been hiding in the Forbidden Forest.

____ Harry has his hearing at the Ministry of Magic for using magic outside of Hogwarts.

____ Umbridge is appointed High Inquisitor.

____ Harry, Ron, Hermione, Ginny, Neville and Luna travel to the Department of Mysteries after Harry has a vision of Sirius being tortured by Voldemort there.

____ Dumbledore's Army holds its first meeting.

____ Azkaban experiences a mass breakout, which includes the escape of Bellatrix Lestrange.

____ Harry saves Dudley and himself from dementors.

____ Harry discovers what's been pulling the seemingly horseless carriages.

Imelda Staunton as Professor Umbridge, Emma Thompson as Professor Trelawney and Maggie Smith as Professor McGonagall in *Harry Potter and the Order of the Phoenix* (2007).

The Heads of Hogwarts

The *Harry Potter* saga and *wizardingworld.com* mention
10 headmasters and headmistresses of Hogwarts:
Can you match their names with their descriptions?

A. Severus Snape

B. Albus Dumbledore

C. Dilys Derwent

D. Phineas Nigellus Black

E. Armando Dippet

F. Minerva McGonagall

G. Dexter Fortescue

H. Dolores Umbridge

I. Eupraxia Mole

J. Everard

1. _____

In 1741, she left St. Mungo's to serve as headmistress of Hogwarts until 1768. Upon learning Arthur is injured, Headmaster Albus Dumbledore asks her to go between the headmaster's office and her other portrait at St. Mungo's.

2. _____

In his portrait, this headmaster can be found speaking loudly and using the same ear trumpet he used in life. His descendant owned an ice cream store in Diagon Alley.

3. _____

Became famous for the deal she made with Hogwarts poltergeist Peeves in 1876, as a result of which he agreed to stop causing havoc in exchange for a once-weekly swim in the boys' toilets, stale bread from the kitchen to throw and a custom-made hat from Madame Bonhabille (a French witch and hat-maker based in Paris).

4. _____

This headmaster uses his multiple portraits to warn Minerva McGonagall that Rufus Scrimgeour is on his way to Hogwarts from the Ministry of Magic after Dumbledore's death.

Michael Gambon as Albus Dumbledore in *Harry Potter and the Order of the Phoenix* (2007).

5. _____

This headmaster has a portrait hanging in the Order of the Phoenix's headquarters at 12 Grimmauld Place.

6. _____

During his time as headmaster, the Chamber of Secrets—created by Hogwarts founder Salazar Slytherin—is opened by Tom Riddle, unleashing the Basilisk within.

7. _____

She serves as headmistress of Hogwarts for a short period of time in 1996 after exposing Dumbledore's Army and being appointed by the Ministry through Educational Decree Number 28.

8. _____

This headmaster witnessed Sybill Trelawney, who had been hoping to be hired as a Divination professor at Hogwarts, make a prophecy about the birth of a child who would defeat the Dark Lord.

9. _____

During his tenure, Death Eaters Alecto and Amycus Carrow are appointed deputy heads.

10. _____

Following the Battle of Hogwarts, she undertakes the task of rebuilding the school and ensuring every student who was denied access by the Death Eaters is allowed to resume their studies.

The Exploding Snap Test

Exploding Snap is a simple game of spotting pairs with the added twist of magical incendiary devices–this version tests your logic with explosive results!

AFTER BEING bamboozled by the wizard chess puzzles, Gryffindor's smartest student has devised a way to get revenge: bewitching an Exploding Snap deck to arrange itself into patterned sequences of nine cards, eight faceup and one facedown. If you can follow the patterned rows and guess the hidden cards, you win! If not, the cards will self-destruct!

Emma Watson
as Hermione
Granger.

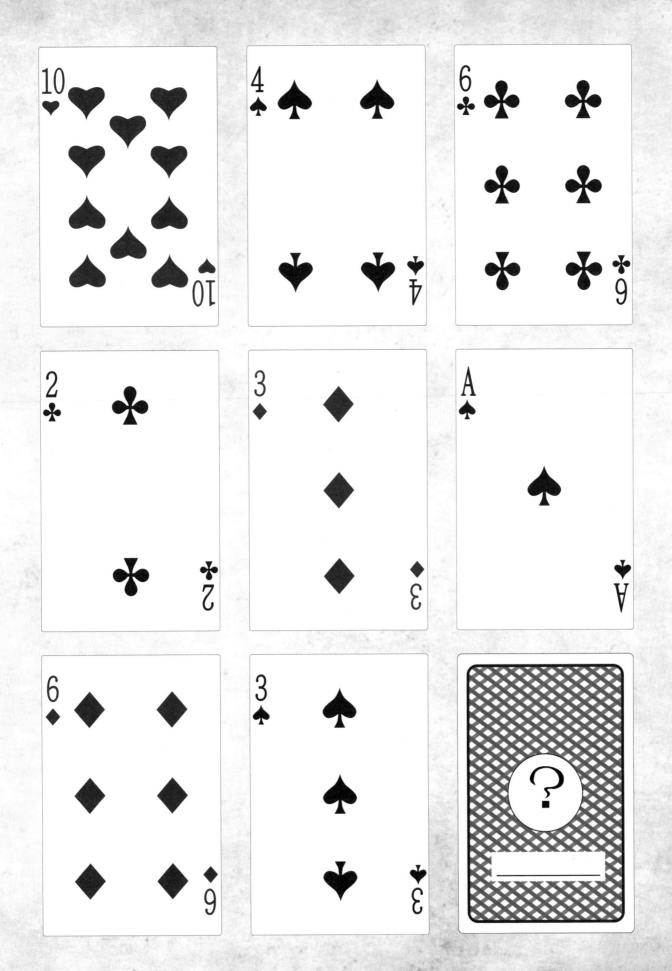

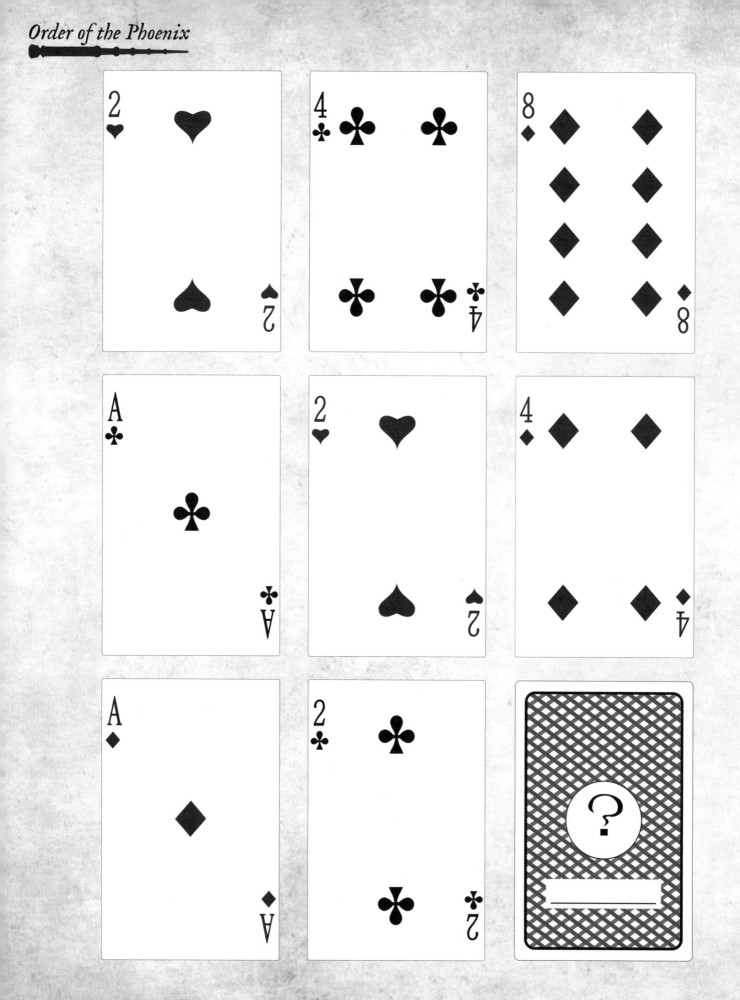

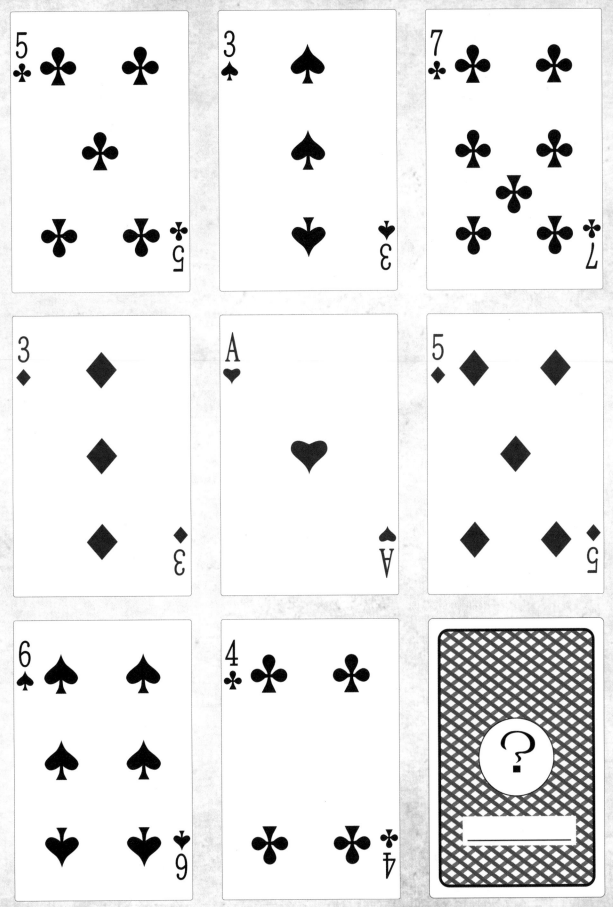

Teacher of the Year

1. What was Umbridge's job before becoming a professor at Hogwarts?
  A. Senior Undersecretary to the Minister for Magic
  B. Head of the Muggle-Born Registration Commission
  C. Senior Undersecretary to the Head of Magical Law Enforcement
  D. Head of the Office for the Detection and Confiscation of Counterfeit Defensive Spells and Protective Objects

2. How many Educational Decrees did the Ministry issue in total during Umbridge's tenure at Hogwarts?
  A. 100   B. 28   C. 40   D. 36

3. Which Hogwarts House was Umbridge in while a student? _____

4. Name all the students mentioned by name Umbridge appointed to the Inquisitorial Squad:
  (1) _____
  (2) _____
  (3) _____
  (4) _____
  (5) _____
  (6) _____
  (7) _____

5. What is the title of the book Umbridge assigned to her Defense Against the Dark Arts class?
  A. *Applied Defensive Magic*
  B. *Theoretical Defensive Magic*
  C. *Defensive Magical Theory*
  D. *Defensive Magical Education*

6. Which incantation did Lee Jordan use to get Nifflers into Umbridge's office window?

  _____

7. What did Umbridge ban the use of in her DADA classes?
  A. Curses   B. Textbooks
  C. Wands   D. Quills

8. What potion were the fifth-year students making while Dolores Umbridge was inspecting Professor Snape's Potions class?

  _____

9. Which Educational Decree made Umbridge Hogwarts High Inquisitor?

  _____

10. Which Educational Decree gives Dolores Umbridge her position as a Hogwarts professor?

  _____

Professor Umbridge

Decrees of Separation

Can you tell the difference between Umbridge's real Educational Decrees and the false? Use the space provided to reveal the ones that aren't telling lies.

👉 No. 1

In the event of the current headmaster being unable to provide a candidate for a teaching post, the Ministry should select an appropriate person.

👉 No. 2

The Inquisitorial Squad may award and remove House points in any manner they see fit.

👉 No. 3

The High Inquisitor may administer Veritaserum whenever she sees fit in order to maintain order and uphold the rules at Hogwarts.

👉 No. 4

No student organization, society, team, group or club may exist without the knowledge and approval of the High Inquisitor.

Did You Know?

The phone number Arthur Weasley dials on the keypad to enter the Ministry of Magic, 62442, spells "magic."

☞ No. 5

Teachers are hereby banned from giving students any information that is not strictly related to the subjects they are paid to teach.

☞ No. 6

No student may travel to Hogsmeade without the approval of the High Inquisitor.

☞ No. 7

Any student found in possession of the magazine *The Quibbler* will be expelled.

☞ No. 8

The High Inquisitor may oversee the grading practices of any subject taught at Hogwarts and adjust these practices when required.

☞ No. 9

Dolores Jane Umbridge (High Inquisitor) has replaced Albus Dumbledore as Head of Hogwarts School of Witchcraft and Wizardry.

☞ No. 10

Any student promoting rumors, lies and propaganda about He-Who-Must-Not-Be-Named's return will be expelled.

REAL DECREES:

Imelda Staunton as Dolores Umbridge in *Harry Potter and the Order of the Phoenix* (2007).

Ho-Ho-Hogwarts:
How did Ollivander find wood for his products?
HE WENT WAND-ERING.

Daniel Radcliffe as Harry Potter in *Harry Potter and the Order of the Phoenix* (2007).

Dementors in Surrey

Can you help Harry and Dudley navigate Little Whinging?

START

END

The Ministry of Magic

Harry has had a vision of Arthur Weasley in grave danger at the Ministry of Magic. Can you help navigate the labyrinthine building to find him?

START

END

The entrance hall to the
Ministry of Magic as seen in
*Harry Potter and the Order
of the Phoenix* (2007).

Ho-Ho-Hogwarts:

What do you call a
Dark wizard caught in
a lightning storm?
VOLT-DEMORT.

MuggleNet's Expert Trivia

YEAR FIVE

You must have been paying close attention to every
word of the saga if you can answer all of these questions.

1. Which Care of Magical Creatures
professor retired with only his arm and
part of a leg intact?

_____

2. Name the caretaker employed while
Molly Weasley was in school.

_____

3. In 1992, Mortlake was questioned about
the experimental charming of what animals?

_____

4. How many Gryffindor students signed
the initial sign-up sheet in the Hog's Head
to be a member of Dumbledore's Army?

_____

5. According to the terms of which
Educational Decree was Professor
Trelawney sacked?

_____

6. Upon entering the Hall of Prophecy
from the Time Room, which row shelf is
directly in front of you?

_____

7. Which charm was used frequently in the
Hogwarts hallways during Harry's fifth year?

_____

8. Which potion did Harry make during
his fifth year that was intentionally dropped
and broken by Professor Snape?

_____

9. What shrub do fifth-year students need
to write an essay on for Herbology class?

_____

10. Hagrid shows (some) of his fifth-year
Care of Magical Creatures students
which animal?

_____

Dumbledore's Army meets in the Room of Requirement in *Harry Potter and the Order of the Phoenix* (2007).

YEAR SIX

HARRY POTTER

and the

HALF-BLOOD PRINCE

Dumbledore finally begins opening up to Harry
during his sixth year, just before his tragic demise.

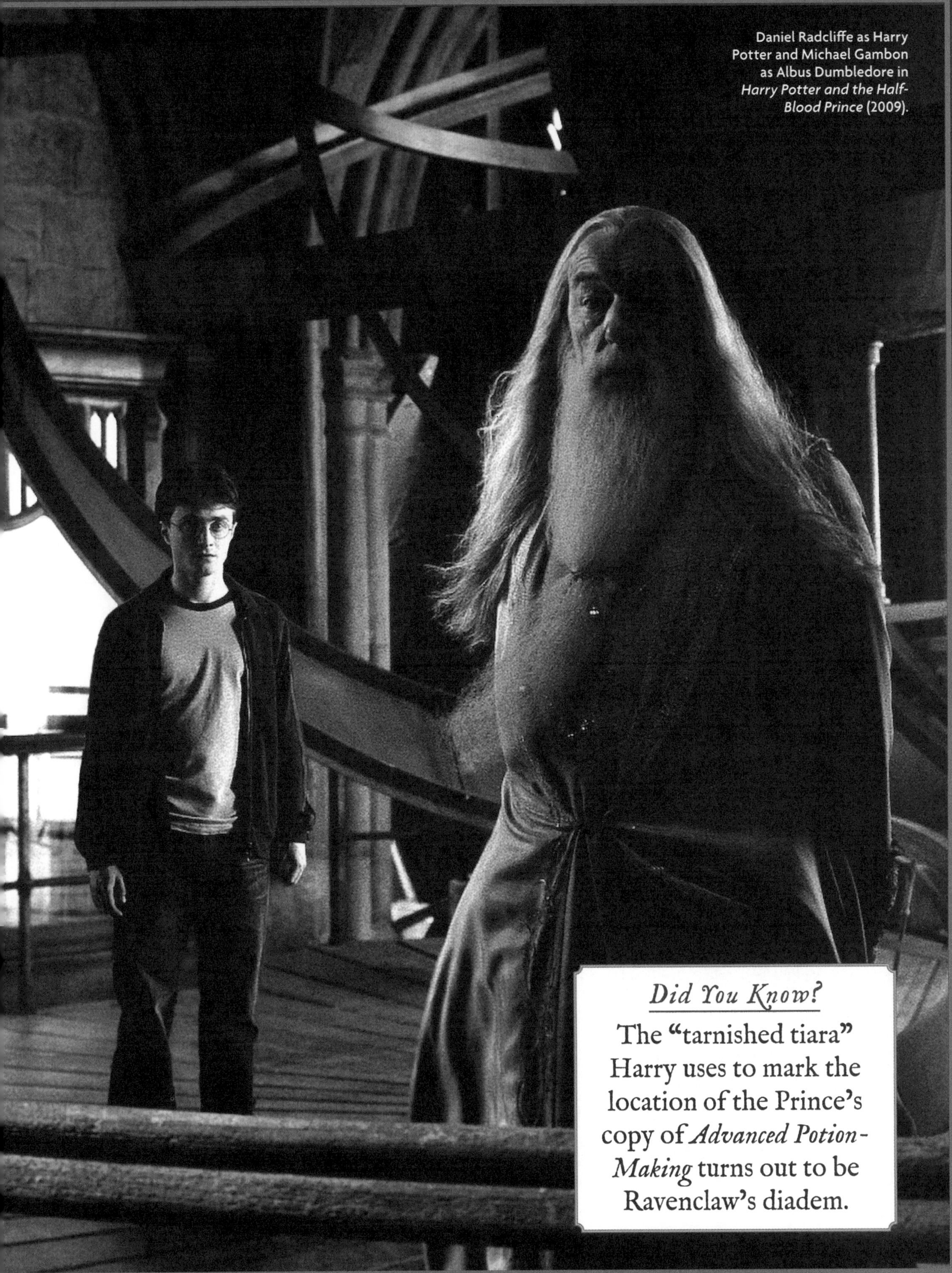

Did You Know?

The "tarnished tiara"
Harry uses to mark the
location of the Prince's
copy of *Advanced Potion-
Making* turns out to be
Ravenclaw's diadem.

The Location Code

In the sixth installment of the *Harry Potter* saga, Harry sees more of the wizarding world beyond Hogwarts than ever before. Can you unscramble the locations pertinent to *Harry Potter and the Half-Blood Prince* with the help of the following clues?

Helena Bonham Carter as Bellatrix Lestrange and Alan Rickman as Severus Snape in *Harry Potter and the Half-Blood Prince* (2009).

1. When Harry arrives here in *Harry Potter and the Half-Blood Prince*, all the hands on the location's unique clock are pointed toward "mortal peril."
HET BRUWOR

_____

2. Although a house on the outskirts of this village appears in *Harry Potter and the Goblet of Fire*, the town isn't described until the sixth installment of the saga.
TLIELT AHNLOTNEG

_____

3. Harry inherits a property on this London thoroughfare at the beginning of the book.
GIRMAMLUD APLEC

_____

4. At the beginning of the book, Snape meets with Narcissa Malfoy and Bellatrix Lestrange in a house on this street.
ISPNENR'S NED

_____

5. In a callback to the first book, Harry and Draco meet in a Diagon Alley shop owned by this witch.
AMDAM ALMIKN

_____

6. This store, owned by someone we later learn is imprisoned at Malfoy Manor, closes in the sixth installment.
LOLIVENADRS

_____

7. Fred and George harbored plans to buy this Hogsmeade joke shop until Hogwarts students' trips to the village were canceled.
ONOKZ'S

_____

8. When Narcissa Malfoy encounters Harry, Ron and Hermione shopping at a clothing store in Diagon Alley, she threatens to take her business to this other boutique.
WITLTIFT NAD TTATNIG'S

_____

Hogwarts Curriculum

YEAR SIX

How closely were you paying attention to the *Harry Potter* books and films?

1. The actor who plays a young Voldemort at the orphanage is related to Ralph Fiennes, who plays the adult iteration, in real life. What is the younger actor's relation to the older?
   A. Son
   B. Nephew
   C. Cousin

2. Which scene was added to the *Half-Blood Prince* movie that wasn't in the book?
   A. The Death Eater battle at the Burrow
   B. The Slug Club Christmas party
   C. The Felix Felicis scene

3. While reading the script for *Half-Blood Prince*, J.K. Rowling had to correct a line because it incorrectly assumed:
   A. Dumbledore was heterosexual
   B. Bellatrix had no children
   C. The Half-Blood Prince was evil

4. *Half-Blood Prince* is the first movie to:
   A. Show Voldemort as Tom Riddle
   B. Show Harry spending Christmas somewhere other than Hogwarts
   C. Not feature a Defense Against the Dark Arts class

Hero Fiennes Tiffin as young Tom Riddle.

Did You Know?
The Elder Wand's core
is a Thestral hair.

Hogwarts Curriculum

Continued

YEAR SIX

How closely were you paying attention to the *Harry Potter* books and films?

5. What was the movie's tagline?
   A. Dark secrets revealed
   B. The rebellion begins
   C. Nowhere is safe

6. How many girls did Jessie Cave best in the audition process to land the role of Lavender Brown?
   A. 10,000
   B. 8,000
   C. 7,000

7. Professor Slughorn's office looks a little familiar. What room did Slughorn's office appear as in the fifth movie?
   A. Dumbledore's office
   B. Room of Requirement
   C. The Defense Against the Dark Arts classroom

8. Director David Yates based his lighting schemes and color palette on the paintings of which Dutch master?

_____

9. The spell _____, used in *Harry Potter and the Half-Blood Prince*, is "for enemies."

10. _____ can be used as an incantation to fill the ears of those around you with an uncontrollable buzzing.

11. When in need of an impromptu fire extinguisher, the spell _____ will do the trick.

Ho-Ho Hogwarts:
Why was Mad-Eye Moody an ineffective teacher?

HE COULDN'T CONTROL HIS PUPILS.

ALBUM/ALAMY

Emma Watson as Hermione Granger in *Harry Potter and the Half-Blood Prince* (2009).

Hogwarts Curriculum

Continued

YEAR SIX

How closely were you paying attention to the *Harry Potter* books and films?

12. Apart from Peeves, the incantation *Langlock* is used by Harry on which other Hogwarts character?

_____

13. Snape saves Draco from a powerful dark spell with the countercurse _____.

14. Can you match the event to the chapter of *Half-Blood Prince* in which it occurred?

Event:

A. Romilda Vane tries to slip Harry a love potion.

B. Ron, Harry, Hermione and Ginny visit Fred and George's new shop.

C. Rufus Scrimgeour takes over for Cornelius Fudge.

D. Dumbledore and Harry arrive back at Hogwarts to find the Dark Mark.

E. Snape makes an Unbreakable Vow.

F. The Pensieve makes its first appearance.

G. Harry first says that Draco has become a Death Eater.

Chapter:

1. __ The Other Minister

2. __ Spinner's End

3. __ Draco's Detour

4. __ The Slug Club

5. __ The House of Gaunt

6. __ The Unbreakable Vow

7. __ The Lightning-Struck Tower

Did You Know?

According to Gamp's Law of Elemental Transfiguration, there are five things that can't be transfigured.

Pensieve Lessons

What better way to learn from past experiences than to relive them as a fly on the wall? If only you had a Pensieve for this quiz.

Michael Gambon as Albus Dumbledore and Daniel Radcliffe as Harry Potter in *Harry Potter and the Half -Blood Prince* (2009).

1. Harry and Dumbledore's first trip into the Pensieve sees them visit the village of _____ _____ with Bob Ogden.

2. Ogden uses the _____ Jinx to stop Marvolo Gaunt from harming his daughter.

3. What ability does Tom Riddle admit he has to Dumbledore before he leaves the orphanage?

_____

4. Dumbledore reveals Voldemort used a memory modifying charm on his uncle Morfin during one of his collected memories. Who is the only other character confirmed to have used this spell?

_____

5. What words did Professor Slughorn add to the end of his memory in which Riddle asks about Horcruxes, tampering with it to cover his tracks?

_____ ____ _____, ___, ____ __ _____

6. From whom does Voldemort acquire Slytherin's Locket and Hufflepuff's Cup?

_____ _____

Michael Gambon as Albus Dumbledore in *Harry Potter and the Goblet of Fire* (2005).

Did You Know?

The Pensieve at Hogwarts has been available for use by the headmaster for as long as the school has existed.

The Horcrux Chronicles

Can you remember the pertinent facts about
the fate of each bit of Tom Riddle's soul?

1. Thinking that _____ was the safest place possible for his first experiment in Horcrux-making, Tom Riddle turned his _____ into a Horcrux. Though this artifact would eventually make its way into the hands of a wealthy private collector, it would be surreptitiously placed with the school books of first-year student _____ _____, setting a petrifying chain of events in motion.

———— ◆ ————

2. Searching out items imbued with personal history, Voldemort finds a _____ belonging to his grandfather _____ _____ and turns it into a Horcrux. Unbeknownst to him, however, this item is also a _____ _____.

3. When Voldemort went searching for relics of the Hogwarts founders to turn into Horcruxes, he found two at once: a _____ belonging to Helga _____ and a locket belonging to _____ _____, the founder of his Hogwarts House.

———————•••———————

4. Using his charm on the ghost of _____ Tower, ___ _____ _____, Voldemort is able to convince her to lead him to a _____ belonging to another Hogwarts founder. He then turns this into a Horcrux that is eventually destroyed by Death Eater incompetence.

———————•••———————

5. Voldemort also created two Horcruxes out of _____ creatures. The first was his snake, _____, who was transformed into a Horcrux thanks to the killing of _____ _____. Voldemort is unaware of having created the second, _____ _____, but he did so on the night of October 31, 1981.

Coded Common Room Passwords

Can you break the codes and provide a forgetful student with the next six passwords to the Gryffindor common room?

GRYFFINDOR'S MOST forgetful student has had to sleep out in the hallway once or twice because the password slipped his mind. As a result, he's been provided with a list of the passwords to Gryffindor Tower for the next six weeks. But just in case they fall into the wrong hands, the passwords have been encoded. Can you crack each one to gain entry?

Ho-Ho Hogwarts

Why did the book critic dislike Nearly Headless Nick?

HE WAS A POORLY EXECUTED CHARACTER.

Rupert Grint as Ron Weasley in *Harry Potter and the Half-Blood Prince* (2009).

1. K M X S T   J V M K Y Z E U

_ _ _ _ _   _ _ _ _ _ _ _ _

Hint: In *Sorcerer's Stone*, Percy Weasley is the
first person Harry hears use this password.

2. ULUS BNIM MOAI ITXM MELB

Hint: This password is an herbological
reference to a type of cactus.

3. NAMA UROJ TROF

Hint: This Latin-derived password
translates to "greater fortune."

4. TOWIB ZWUVGH

_ _ _ _ _   _ _ _ _ _ _

Hint: This password appears in
Chapter 22 of *Goblet of Fire*.

5. SKOD NIBD IDSO

Hint: This password is used in the same chapter in which
Harry begins his Patronus lessons with Professor Lupin.

6. SH AD ER DL BA

Hint: This password is also the name
of a popular Muggle board game.

MuggleNet's Expert Trivia

YEAR SIX

You must have been paying close attention to every word of the saga if you can answer all of these questions.

1. Which educational decree number makes Dolores Umbridge the new Headmistress of Hogwarts?

_____

2. In the Hufflepuff common room, what is Helga Hufflepuff's portrait doing?

_____

3. What is Professor Grubbly-Plank's first name?

_____

4. What food did Dumbledore enjoy with Lupin when inviting him to study at Hogwarts?

_____

5. Which potion did Draco make for Professor Slughorn when tasked to create something "amusing"?

_____

6. In what year did Slughorn become Potions Master after returning to Hogwarts?

_____

7. Which creature is of Japanese origin but mistakenly identified by Professor Snape as being from Mongolia?

_____

8. Which book did Snape claim that Hermione's answer to his question about non-verbal spells was taken from almost verbatim?

_____

9. Which wizard, whose portrait hangs in Hogwarts, is thought to have been one of the Knights of the Round Table?

_____

10. Who is the founder of the Leaky Cauldron?

_____

Richard Leaf as John Dawlish, Imelda Staunton as Dolores Umbridge, Robert Hardy as Cornelius Fudge and George Harris as Kinglsey Shacklebolt in *Harry Potter and the Order of the Phoenix* (2007). After her time as Headmistress of Hogwarts, Umbridge returns to the Ministry.

The Noble and Most Ancient House of Black

Their motto is "Toujours Pur," and they won't let anyone forget it. Can you fill in the blanks on the Black family tree?

Daniel Radcliffe as Harry Potter and Gary Oldman as Sirius Black in front of the Black family tree at 12 Grimmauld Place.

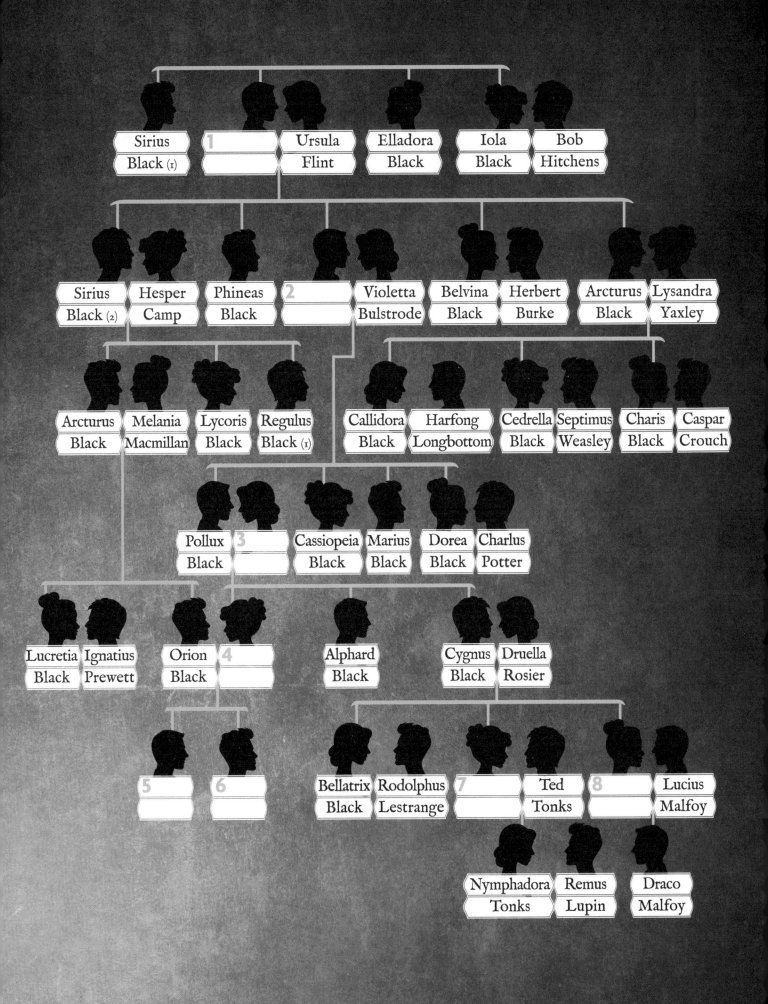

The Half-Blood Prince's Textbook

Can you remember these expert-level bits
of trivia from the story of Harry and Snape?

1. In the chapter "Birthday Surprises," Harry is disappointed to find that the Prince had made no notes on:
  A. Golpalott's Third Law
  B. Gamp's Fifth Law
  C. Dagworth's Second Law
  D. Galician's Fourth Law

2. What is the counter-jinx to *Levicorpus?*
  A. *Levicorpus*
  B. *Descecorpus*
  C. *Liberacorpus*
  D. *Tombecorpus*

3. Who invented the incantation *Langlock?*
  A. Albus Dumbledore
  B. Newt Scamander
  C. James Potter
  D. Severus Snape

4. On the day of Hermione's Apparition test, Harry makes the Prince's heavily corrected version of which potion?
  A. Hiccoughing Solution
  B. Cheering Draught
  C. Draught of Peace
  D. Elixir to Induce Euphoria

5. When finished, what shade of yellow is the Elixir to Induce Euphoria?
  A. Mustard
  B. Sunshine
  C. Butter
  D. Daffodil

6. Harry hides *Advanced Potion-Making* in a cupboard in the Room of Requirement, next to a skeleton with how many legs?
  A. 1   B. 3   C. 5   D. 7

7. According to Snape's notes, the incantation *Sectumsempra* should be used against whom?
   A. Muggles
   B. Werewolves
   C. Enemies
   D. James Potter

Alan Rickman as Severus Snape in *Harry Potter and the Half-Blood Prince* (2009).

8. According to Slughorn, which ingredient counterbalances the side effects of the Elixir to Induce Euphoria?
   A. Cheese
   B. Boomslang skin
   C. Peppermint
   D. Honey

9. What was Snape's self-given moniker the "Half-Blood Prince" inspired by?
   A. His godfather
   B. His favorite teacher
   C. A famous potioneer
   D. His mother's maiden name

10. Harry used the incantation *Levicorpus* on which one of his friends?
   A. Ron
   B. Neville
   C. Luna
   D. Hermione

Did You Know?
Before earning a place at the Royal Academy of Dramatic Arts, Alan Rickman was the cofounder of a graphic design studio.

The Lions of Gryffindor

It might take some brain racking to remember the names of every player to compete for Gryffindor during Harry's time at Hogwarts. Can you name them in the spaces opposite?

NAME:	YEARS:
1.	1-3, 5
2.	5
3.	1-3, 5
4.	6
5.	6
6.	6
7.	1-3, 5
8.	1-3, 5
9.	5-6
10.	6
11.	5
12.	1-3, 5-6
13.	1-3
14.	5-6
15.	6

YEAR SEVEN

HARRY POTTER

and the

DEATHLY HALLOWS

(and beyond)

Instead of studying for his N.E.W.T.s by the
common room fire, Harry spends what should
be his final year at Hogwarts hunting Horcruxes.

Did You Know?

Professor Trelawney states in *Prisoner of Azkaban* that when 13 dine together, the first to rise is the first to die. When 13 people share a bottle of firewhisky after the Battle of the Seven Potters, Lupin is the first to leave and, eventually, the first of the group to die.

The Seven Potters

We give you the mode of transport and the
bodyguard—can you remember the Harry Potter decoy?

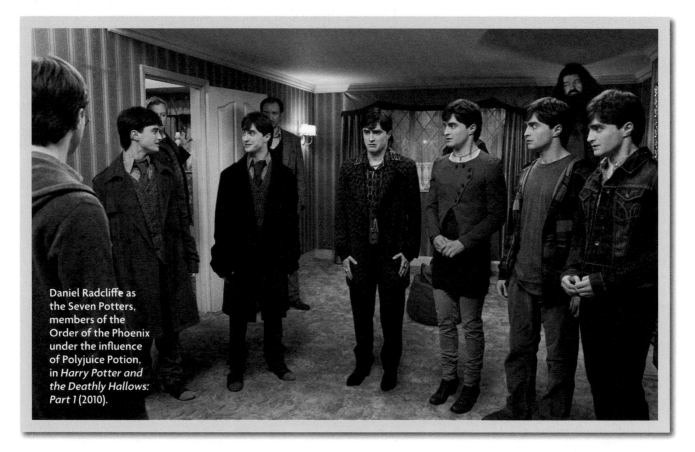

Daniel Radcliffe as
the Seven Potters,
members of the
Order of the Phoenix
under the influence
of Polyjuice Potion,
in *Harry Potter and
the Deathly Hallows:
Part 1* (2010).

1. Thestral, with Kingsley Shacklebolt _____

2. Broomstick, with Arthur Weasley _____

3. Thestral, with Bill Weasley _____

4. Broomstick, with Mad-Eye Moody _____

5. Motorbike, with Hagrid _____

6. Broomstick, with Tonks _____

7. Broomstick, with Lupin _____

Robbie Coltrane as Rubeus Hagrid and Daniel Radcliffe as Harry Potter in *Harry Potter and the Deathly Hallows: Part 1* (2010).

Dumbledore's Will

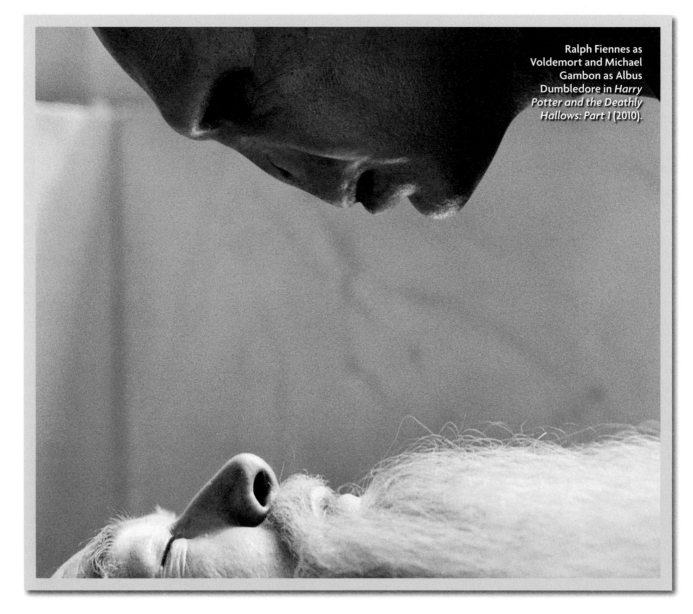

Ralph Fiennes as Voldemort and Michael Gambon as Albus Dumbledore in *Harry Potter and the Deathly Hallows: Part 1* (2010).

PICTURELUX/THE HOLLYWOOD ARCHIVE/ALAMY

1. The Last Will and Testament of Albus _____ _____ _____ Dumbledore:

2. To Ronald _____ Weasley, I leave my _____, in the hope that he will _____ ___ when he uses it.

3. To Miss Hermione _____ Granger, I leave my _____ of ____ _____ __ _____ _____ _____, in the hope that she will find it _____ and _____.

4. To Harry _____ Potter, I leave the _____ he _____ in his first _____ _____ at Hogwarts, as a reminder of the rewards of _____ and _____.

Your N.E.W.T Exams

YEAR SEVEN

Use your comprehensive knowledge from the past seven years at Hogwarts to see if you can master this expert-level grab bag of wizarding knowledge.

1. What is the only one of the Five Principal Exceptions to Gamp's Law of Elemental Transfiguration mentioned explicitly in the *Harry Potter* series? _____

2. In J.K. Rowling's original notes, the subject of Transfiguration was rendered as Transfiguration/_____.

3. Where do vanished objects go? _____

4. The first recorded Animagus in wizarding history was Falco Aesalon, a wizard from which country? _____

5. What is the incantation for the charm Harry casts between Molly Weasley and Voldemort during the Battle of Hogwarts? _____

Ho-Ho Hogwarts

Why did Snape throw away his old potions?

THEY WERE PAST THEIR HEX-PIRATION DATES.

Daniel Radcliffe as Harry Potter in *Harry Potter and the Deathly Hallows: Part 1* (2010).

Your N.E.W.T Exams
Continued

YEAR SEVEN

Use your comprehensive knowledge from the past seven years at Hogwarts to see if you can master this expert-level grab bag of wizarding knowledge.

6. *Capacious Extremis* is the incantation for which charm, used by Hermione in *Harry Potter and the Deathly Hallows?*

_____

7. *Anapneo* is a spell used by which Hogwarts professor to allow a student to breathe? _____

8. This incantation can be used to stop a falling object. _____

9. A Caterwauling Charm is used by Death Eaters near which wizarding establishment to catch people out after curfew?

_____

10. What is the incantation for the Blasting Curse, used by Hermione in an attempt to kill Nagini?

_____

Did You Know?
The book Hermione consults for information on the Deathly Hallows symbol is *Spellman's Syllabary.*

ALBUM/ALAMY

Rupert Grint as Ron Weasley, Emma Watson as Hermione Granger and Daniel Radcliffe as Harry Potter in *Harry Potter and the Deathly Hallows: Part 2* (2011).

Your N.E.W.T Exams

Continued

YEAR SEVEN

Use your comprehensive knowledge from the past seven years at Hogwarts to see if you can master this expert-level grab bag of wizarding knowledge.

11. Which spell does Harry use to carve Dobby's epitaph?

_____

12. This healing essence used in *Harry Potter and the Deathly Hallows* is based on a real herbal anti-inflammatory.

_____

13. The use of this potion is described by Horace Slughorn as illegal in competitions.

_____

14. During preparation for N.E.W.T.s in their sixth year, Harry and Hermione study these potions, which can magically refill themselves indefinitely. _____

15. Who wrote *Advanced Potion-Making?* _____

Ho-Ho Hogwarts

How does Voldemort enter a room?

HE SLITHERS IN.

Josh Herdman as Gregory
Goyle and Tom Felton as Draco
Malfoy in *Harry Potter and the
Deathly Hallows: Part 2* (2011).

Your N.E.W.T Exams

Continued

YEAR SEVEN

Use your comprehensive knowledge from the past seven years at Hogwarts to see if you can master this expert-level grab bag of wizarding knowledge.

16. Hermione and Harry use this spell to repel hexes from their temporary campsites in *Harry Potter and the Deathly Hallows.*

_____

17. This curse was used by Mad-Eye to protect 12 Grimmauld Place against Snape. _____

18. Which spell does Lupin fear will give Harry away to the Death Eaters?

_____

19. Who is the first member of the Order of the Phoenix to kill a witch or wizard with *Avada Kedavra* in the series? _____

20. How many Galleons does the reward for the capture of Harry reach at its peak?

_____

Did You Know?

To study N.E.W.T.-level Transfiguration, Professor McGonagall requires an O.W.L. score of Exceeds Expectations.

Daniel Radcliffe as Harry Potter, Rupert Grint as Ron Weasley and Emma Watson as Hermione Granger in *Harry Potter and the Deathly Hallows: Part 1* (2010).

Escape From Malfoy Manor

During the Second Wizarding War, the Malfoys keep
a private prison at the behest of Lord Voldemort.
Can you escape before the Dark Lord arrives?

Jason Isaacs as Lucius Malfoy, Helen McCrory as
Narcissa Malfoy and Tom Felton as Draco Malfoy in
Harry Potter and the Deathly Hallows: Part 1 (2010).

START

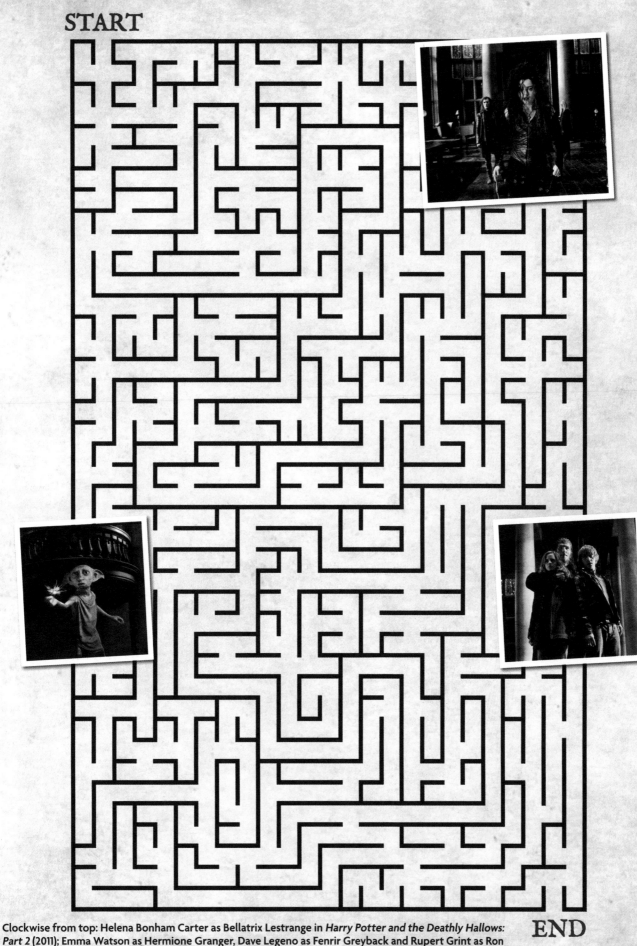

Clockwise from top: Helena Bonham Carter as Bellatrix Lestrange in *Harry Potter and the Deathly Hallows: Part 2* (2011); Emma Watson as Hermione Granger, Dave Legeno as Fenrir Greyback and Rupert Grint as Ron Weasley in *Harry Potter and the Deathly Hallows: Part 2* (2011); Dobby (voiced by Toby Jones) in *Harry Potter and the Deathly Hallows: Part 1* (2010).

END

The Tale of the Three Brothers

This wizarding fairy tale is the key to understanding the Deathly Hallows. How well do you know it?

Emma Watson as Hermione Granger, Rupert Grint as Ron Weasley, Daniel Radcliffe as Harry Potter and Rhys Ifans as Xenophilius Lovegood in *Harry Potter and the Deathly Hallows: Part 1* (2010).

1. "The Tale of the Three Brothers" can be found in
The Tales of _____ _____ _____.

2. When Hermione reads it aloud, Ron interrupts, taking issue
with the setting. His mother always said the brothers were
walking at _____ , rather than _____.

3. The three brothers cheated Death by magically creating a
_____ , so they could cross a _____.

4. Death gifted the first brother with the most _____
_____ in existence. It can _____ duels for its owner.

5. The second brother requested a means of recalling loved ones
from the dead. He was given the _____ Stone.

6. More humble than his other brothers, the third brother asked
for a way to _____ Death. Death gave the brother his _____
___ _____.

7. The first brother was murdered and had his wand stolen
___ days after receiving it.

8. After turning the Stone _____ times in his hand, the
second brother was reunited with his deceased lover, but there
was a _____ between them. In despair, he killed himself.

9. Years later, the third brother _____ Death like an
_____ _____ and gave the Cloak to _____ _____.

A True Gryffindor

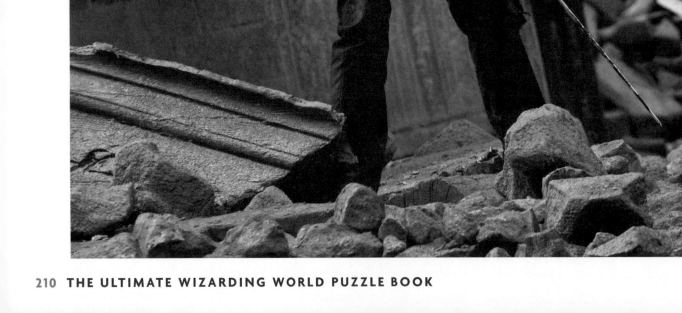

Matthew Lewis as Neville Longbottom in *Harry Potter and the Deathly Hallows: Part 2* (2011).

Neville's big moment comes at the Battle of Hogwarts.
Can you spot the six differences in this pivotal scene?

Matthew Lewis as Neville
Longbottom in *Harry
Potter and the Deathly
Hallows: Part 2* (2011).

The United Kingdom of Magic

Can you fill in the magical locations on this map
of the United Kingdom with the help of the clues provided?

1. A running start will get you onto this secret loading dock in the U.K. capital.

2. This wizarding district was filmed at the vast Leadenhall Market in London.

3. The only all-wizard town in Britain.

4. The alma mater of Britain's finest wizards.

5. Hermione's parents once took her on a camping trip to this location in England, where she later hides out with Harry and Ron.

6. The Midlands village in which Severus Snape and Lily Evans grew up.

7. The location where the Minister of Magic visits his Muggle counterpart.

8. The suburban town in which 4 Privet Drive can be found.

9. Harry's ancestral village.

10. The town in which one might find the Burrow.

MuggleNet's Expert Trivia

YEAR SEVEN

You must have been paying close attention to every word of the saga if you can answer all of these questions.

1. Which creatures did Elphias Doge narrowly escape on his world tour?

_____

2. When we meet a wizard known only as Bob, what animal is he holding?

_____

3. Ollivanders: Makers of Fine Wands since _____ B.C.

4. In which classroom does Firenze teach Divination?

_____

5. Which incantation is used to block the target's vision?

_____

6. Which charm did Hermione cast on her beaded bag to carry the trio's supplies?

_____

7. Which charm allows the target object to multiply and make an exact copy?

_____

Rupert Grint as Ron Weasley and Daniel Radcliffe as Harry Potter in *Harry Potter and the Deathly Hallows: Part 2* (2011).

Cursed Catch-Up

Nineteen years after the Battle of Hogwarts, where are our favorite characters at the start of *Cursed Child*?

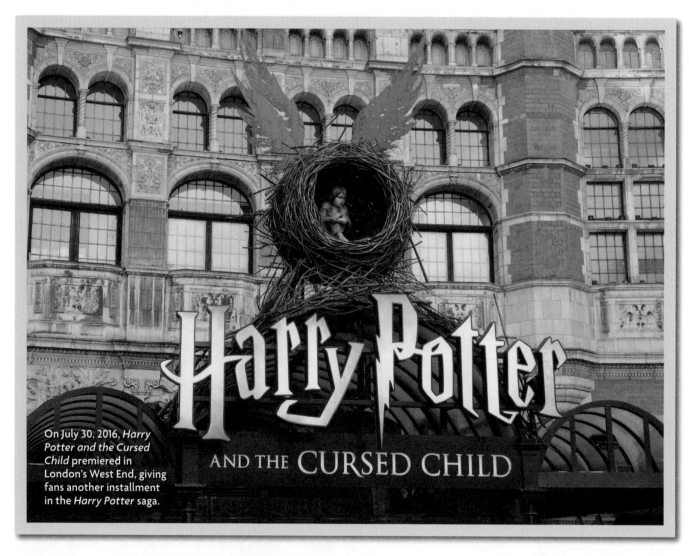

On July 30, 2016, *Harry Potter and the Cursed Child* premiered in London's West End, giving fans another installment in the *Harry Potter* saga.

1. Of which Ministry of Magic Department is Harry the head?
    A. Magical Law Enforcement
    B. International Magical Cooperations
    C. Magical Games and Sports
    D. Magical Transportation

2. Who is the Minister of Magic at the start of *Cursed Child*?
    A. Kingsley Shacklebolt
    B. Hermione Granger
    C. Draco Malfoy
    D. Dedalus Diggle

3. What is Ron's job title 19 years later?
    A. Head of the Auror Office
    B. Head of Misuse of Muggle Artifacts
    C. Stay-at-home dad
    D. Co-owner of Weasleys' Wizard Wheezes

4. Who is the Headmaster/Headmistress of Hogwarts?
    A. Minerva McGonagall
    B. Neville Longbottom
    C. Hannah Abbott
    D. Filius Flitwick

5. What are the names of all the children of Hogwarts Class of 1998 alumni featured in *Cursed Child*?
    A. _____
    B. _____
    C. _____
    D. _____
    E. _____

Jamie Parker as Harry Potter, Noma Dumezweni as Hermione Granger and Paul Thornley as Ron Weasley in costume for *Harry Potter and the Cursed Child.*

Match the Wand Movement

Can you match the spell to its wand movement as seen at the Wizarding World of Harry Potter theme parks and in the Harry Potter mobile games?

1. *Accio*
2. *Fumos*
3. Switching Spell
4. *Aparecium*
5. *Alohomora*
6. *Mimble Wimble*
7. *Impedimenta*

Maggie Smith as Minerva McGonagall in *Harry Potter and the Deathly Hallows: Part 2* (2011).

Eddie Redmayne as Newt Scamander in *Fantastic Beasts: The Crimes of Grindelwald* (2018).

Newt's Case

Can you navigate your way through Newt Scamander's endlessly complicated suitcase to find the right creature?

START

END

A Walk Around Wizarding New York

Can you follow Newt's new American pals as they hurry through the Big Apple?

START

END

ENTERTAINMENT PICTURES/ALAMY

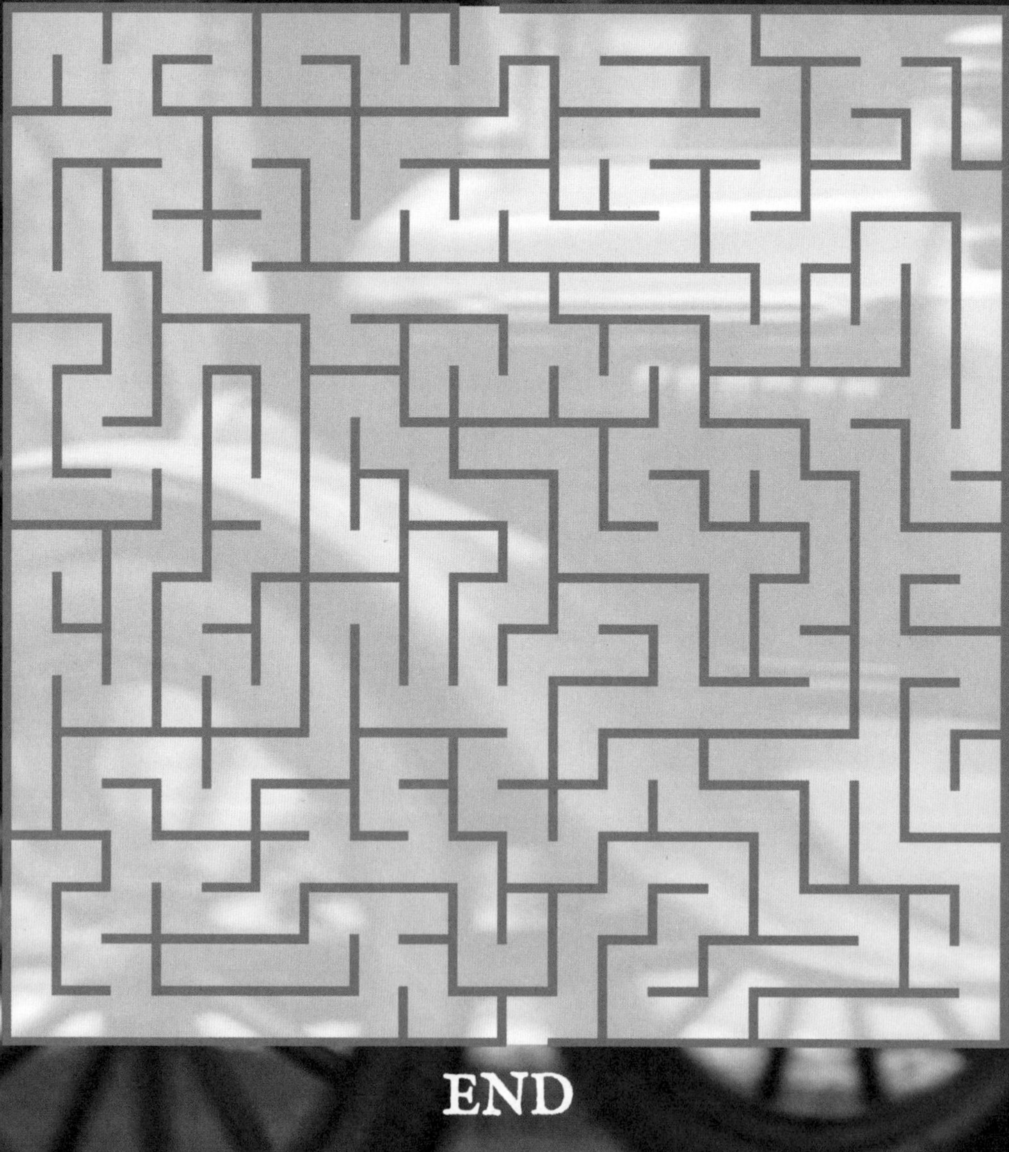

Katherine Waterston as Tina Goldstein and Eddie Redmayne as Newt Scamander in *Fantastic Beasts and Where to Find Them* (2016)

YEAR ONE

FIND YOUR WIZARDING WARES PGS. 8-9

1. The Leaky Cauldron
2. Florean Fortescue's Ice Cream Parlor
3. Ollivanders
4. Quality Quidditch Supplies
5. Flourish and Blotts
6. Madam Malkin's Robes for All Occasions
7. Eeylops Owl Emporium
8. Gringotts

A ROBBERY AT GRINGOTTS

PG. 11

1. 12,750 Galleons–Antique Foe-Glass
2. 16,840 Galleons–Jeweled Pensieve
3. 8,050 Galleons–Original Pressing, Merlin Chocolate Frog Card
4. 14,360 Galleons–Solid Gold Omnioculars
5. 20,000 Galleons–Uncut Sapphires, Rubies and Opals

HOGWARTS CLASS OF '98

PGS. 12-13

Gryffindor:
Harry Potter
Ron Weasley
Neville Longbottom
Dean Thomas
Seamus Finnigan
Hermione Granger
Lavender Brown
Parvati Patil

Ravenclaw:
Anthony Goldstein
Michael Corner
Terry Boot
Padma Patil
Mandy Brocklehurst
Lisa Turpin

Hufflepuff:
Ernie Macmillan
Justin Finch-Fletchley
Wayne Hopkins
Hannah Abbott
Susan Bones

Slytherin:
Draco Malfoy
Vincent Crabbe
Gregory Goyle
Theodore Nott
Blaise Zabini
Pansy Parkinson
Daphne Greengrass
Millicent Bulstrode

CHANGING STAIRS PGS. 14-15

START

END

FIRST-YEAR CURRICULUM

PGS. 16-17

1. Troll
2. *Oculus Reparo*
3. *Locomotor Mortis*
4. *Wingardium Leviosa*
5. Bezoar
6. Wolfsbane
7. Centaur
8. Boarhound
9. Garlic

```
M G Y E U P S R H B M L T R O L L
Y Q A C F Q X Y E C J V D J P D O
D A W H P E D B W B M Y B L A J R
Q K H F N O B L J W E M Z C U Z A
W C Z M U D D J R U D I H M F O Y
W R L V Y U W I S A E B I F H P A
T I J T L C L L K V X W G X Q G U
G S N L P D F O Z C E N T A U R U
L Y B G V J B L Y A Q P G F V S K
O M O T A R N X N O B O G G A A C
C S J D K R H W S I L C S K H C S
O B H M R J D X J W U U D P U E M
M H G P J W K I Z X Y L D Q Y Z R
O E A M Z O Q K U P B U C Q I A T
T Y N B L X I Z M Q S B A H H J
O X L F O V S I Y L R K G Y H I
R Q I B A S I G I F B E L W S M S
M Y C E R B D E Q H U P V F A L C
O F H Z H A L N W W A W I F I A
R J D A O U E S H J A A O X U R S D
T I Z K R N Z R P A Q I H D Q T N A
S W N L D A Y B E P R K G M R J N
```

HOGWARTS CURRICULUM: YEAR ONE PGS. 18-20

1. C. Oxford
2. I show not your face, but your heart's desire
3. A. Hedwig
4. D. Pairs of glasses
5. Tom Riddle
6. Peeves
7. Corned beef
8. Privet Drive
9. Halloween
10. Pumpkin Pasty
11. A. The Dursleys
    B. Mrs. Weasley
    C. Hermione
    D. Hagrid
    E. Dumbledore (anonymously)
12. Dudley
13. Pig
14. *Wingardium Leviosa*
15. *Alohomora*
16. *Petrificus Totalus*

PLOTTING THE PLOT PG. 21

1. B. The Boy Who Lived
2. D. Diagon Alley
3. A. The Sorting Hat
4. F. The Mirror of Erised
5. C. The Forbidden Forest
6. E. The Man With Two Faces

WIZARDING WORDS PGS. 22-23

```
B L S H N W Y S Z P Z Y J B A B F
D G A Z E P B K V O P Z K F H M Z
C Q D K C U H O A M I U K N B A R
G Q M E S R Q E O B V B J X E I Y
L Q N N K J O I X C T B E Z O A R
L Y S Q W I L E R E Y K D Y T O N
I S L I M E R O A E S U E Q Z M R
V H E R A O R Y E I Z D M S B E M
G N P P N B W E O M J K U N G X U
T V R I D A W A W Y L P W N O H G
X Q E W R L P W S O V J T T B F E
Q C C Y A C A C Q X L W K L A U L
K T H P K H S B I W D F E K S M O
S U A F E E X K C H F X O N I I H
W P U Z H M J V J T C S D T L H Z
P A N E D Y P O L T E R G E I S T
F T N P V Z E B T T Y Z J R S Y B
Y W M D V M N C Q Y A N W K K G V
N W U Y L A A Q R T G M H H H R D Z
A D V W F O T U L J M N L D Y E W
X E A J T K R N L Q K R J O M M K
B H V A V C W E P S E S Q A S K I
Q S P E L L B O O K X Y O S N Q V
```

BE THE SORTING HAT PGS. 24-25

1. Slytherin 2. Hufflepuff 3. Gryffindor 4. Ravenclaw

NOTE: *Sometimes the Sorting Hat has a hard time choosing which House a student should be sorted into. These students are called Hatstalls.*

THE FORBIDDEN FOREST PGS. 26-27

START

END

WANDLORE WISDOM PGS. 28-29

1. Harry 2. Draco 3. Ron (#1) 4. Voldemort
5. Bellatrix Lestrange 6. Hermione 7. Ron (#2)
8. Umbridge 9. Peter Pettigrew 10. Viktor Krum

MAGIC SHADOWS: HARRY PGS. 30-31

TEACHER OF THE YEAR: PROFESSOR QUIRRELL PG. 32

1. The Leaky Cauldron 2. Garlic 3. D. Zombie
4. C. Quirinus 5. Oliver Wood 6. D. Muggle Studies
7. B. Unicorn hair 8. The Black Forest
9. C. Ambitious 10. B. Buying a book on vampires

YEAR ONE CONT.

CHECKMATE CHALLENGE
PGS. 34-37

1. Rd8# 2. Qxf7# 3. Nd4 f5#
4. Qh7# 5. Qd8# 6. Nxc4#

MUGGLENET'S EXPERT TRIVIA **PG. 39**

1. Hankerton Humble
2. Minerva McGonagall
3. Herbert Beery
4. Silver Arrow
5. *Impervius*
6. *Rictusempra*
7. Comet Trading Company
8. Growth Charm
9. *Repello Muggletum*
10. Scouring Charm

THIRD-FLOOR CORRIDOR
PGS. 40-41

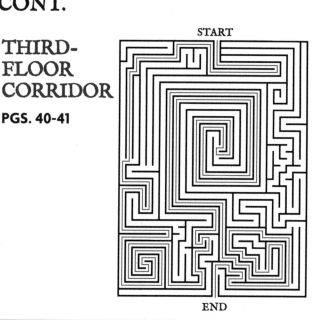

START

END

YEAR TWO

NEW FRIENDS, NEW FOES
PGS. 44-45

1. Aragog
2. Arthur Weasley
3. Colin Creevey
4. Dobby
5. Tom Riddle
6. Lucius Malfoy
7. Mr. Borgin
8. Moaning Myrtle
9. Gilderoy Lockhart

MAGIC SHADOWS: HERMIONE
PGS. 52-53

ARTHUR WEASLEY'S SILLY CIRCUITS **PGS. 46-51**

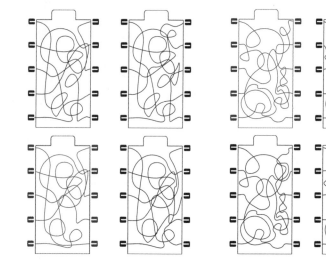

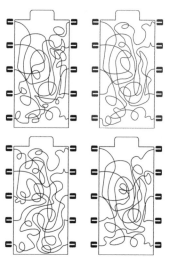

HOGWARTS CURRICULUM: YEAR TWO PGS. 54-59

1. A. 14
2. B. The door to the Chamber of Secrets
3. Vladimir Putin
4. D. "I didn't know you could read."
5. Slytherin's locket
6. B. Hugh Grant
7. C. "Incident on 57th Street"
8. Lacewing flies, leeches, powdered Bicorn horn, knotgrass, fluxweed, shredded Boomslang skin and a bit of the person you want to turn into
9. *Expelliarmus* or Disarming Charm
10. *Immobilus*
11. *Rictusempra*
12. *Serpensortia*
13. *Aparecium*
14. *Vipera Evanesca*
15. *Arania Exumai*
16. *Finite Incantatem*
17. pickled toad; hair; mine; Dark Lord
18. A. Maggoty haggis, D. Fungus-covered peanuts, F. A ghost orchestra featuring a musical saw, H. A grey cake shaped like a tombstone

ARE YOU A QUIDDITCH EXPERT? PGS. 60-61

1. Real	4. Real	7. Real
2. Fake	5. Fake	8. Fake
3. Real	6. Real	Bonus: 700

MATCH DAY LOGIC PGS. 62–63

George Weasley	Alicia Spinnet	Adrian Pucey	Draco Malfoy
Marcus Flint	Quaffle	Katie Bell	Bludger #2
Snitch	Angelina Johnson	Bludger #1	Fred Weasley

ENEMIES OF THE HEIR, BEWARE PGS. 64-65

1. C. Mrs. Norris
2. B. Colin Creevey
3. E. Nearly Headless Nick
4. D. Justin Finch-Fletchley
5. A. Hermione Granger
6. A. Penelope Clearwater

TEACHER OF THE YEAR: PROFESSOR LOCKHART PG. 66

1. B. 7
2. 10
3. D. 5
4. A. Violet
5. Ravenclaw
6. C. Memory Charm
7. B. *Peskipiksi Pesternomi*
8. C. 10
9. B. Dark Force Defense League
10. B. *Playdate With a Poltergeist*

GILDEROY IN PRINT PGS. 68-69

A. *Break with a Banshee*
C. *Gadding with Ghouls*
G. *Holidays with Hags*
I. *Travels with Trolls*
L. *Year with the Yeti*
N. *Marauding with Monsters*

THE RIGHT STUFF PGS. 70-71

Option 1

MUGGLENET'S EXPERT TRIVIA PG. 72

1. Gilderoy Lockhart
2. XXX
3. 437
4. 199
5. Freezing Charm
6. Homorphous Charm
7. Severing Charm
8. Professor Sinistra
9. Circe
10. Yak

WEASLEYS' WIZARDING CLOCK PGS. 74-75

1. Arthur	4. Bill	7. Fred
2. Percy	5. Charlie	8. Ron
3. Ginny	6. Molly	9. George

YEAR THREE

ESCAPE FROM AZKABAN PGS. 78-79

START

END

TEACHER OF THE YEAR: PROFESSOR LUPIN PG. 88

1. A. Boggarts, Hinkypunks, Redcaps, Kappas, grindylows
2. 394
3. D. A and B
4. full moon
5. unregistered Animagi
6. B. Sirius thought Lupin was the spy
7. Mischief Managed, Snape
8. Wolf
9. C. John
10. Richard Harris

HOGWARTS CURRICULUM: YEAR THREE PGS. 80-84

1. B. Write essays
2. A. Newt Scamander
3. C. Both A and B
4. C. Dudley Dursley
5. C. Dumbledore's office
6. A. Pumpkin and Crackerjack
7. *A Brief History of Time* by Stephen Hawking
8. *Lumos*
9. *Riddikulus*, Laughter
10. *Bombarda*
11. C. Despair
12. C. *Waddiwasi*
13. *Impervius*
14. A. *Dissendium*
15. Cheering
16. *Arresto Momentum*
17. The One-Eyed Witch's Hump
18. *Wingardium Leviosa*

HOGSMEADE VILLAGE PG. 90

1. Dervish and Banges
2. The Hog's Head
3. Honeydukes
4. Hogsmeade Station
5. Zonko's Joke Shop
6. The Shrieking Shack
7. The Three Broomsticks
8. Hogsmeade Post Office
9. Madam Puddifoot's Tea Shop

HAGRID'S CARE OF MAGICAL CREATURES QUIZ PGS. 92-93

1. C. Professor Kettleburn
2. A. Harry, Ron and Hermione
3. *The Monster Book of Monsters*
4. B. 12
5. Lettuce
6. C. Draco Malfoy
7. C. Conjunctivitis
8. B. September 1993
9. B. Hippogriff
10. C. Minsk

MAGIC SHADOWS: RON PGS. 86-87

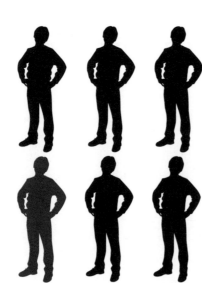

CARE OF MAGICAL CREATURES
PGS. 94-95

1. Blast-Ended Skrewt: A creature created by Hagrid by cross-breeding fire crabs with manticores.
2. Hippogriff: An eagle-horse hybrid that proves essential to a *Prisoner of Azkaban* escape plan.
3. Flobberworm: An objectively boring, herbivorous animal Draco Malfoy claims to have been bitten by.
4. Salamander: Not to be confused with the magic-less animal of the same name, a fire-starting lizard.
5. Niffler: A creature obsessed with shiny objects that becomes a main character in the *Fantastic Beasts* films.
6. Thestral: A horse-like creature invisible to those who have not witnessed death.
7. Unicorn: A creature with magical blood and a single horn on its forehead.

MONSTER BOOK OF WORD JUMBLES **PGS. 96-97**

1. DOXY
2. KAPPA
3. NUNDU
4. DIRICAWL
5. BOGGART
6. BOWTRUCKLE
7. FWOOPER
8. DEMIGUISE
9. GRAPHORN

THE JINXED GOBSTONE **PG. 98**

Put three marbles on each pan—for a total of six marbles on the scale—and leave two marbles off. Compare the six marbles on the scale—if one pan is heavier than the other, you only have to focus on those three. You compare two of those three marbles to each other on the scale. If they are the same weight, the third is the heaviest. If one is heavier than the other, then that's the jinxed one. If, when comparing the six marbles, you find that both sides are equal, then you know the heaviest marble has to be one of the two marbles that are not on the scale. This means you only have to compare those two remaining marbles and you have the heaviest marble in two measurements.

HERMIONE'S IMPOSSIBLE SCHEDULE **PGS. 100-101**

1. Potions
2. Defense Against the Dark Arts
3. Care of Magical Creatures
4. Arithmancy
5. Divination
6. Muggle Studies
7. Herbology
8. Transfiguration
9. Charms
10. Ancient Runes
11. History of Magic
12. Astronomy

THE EYE OF THE SEER **PG. 102**

1. True 2. True 3. False (around Easter)
4. True (Dumbledore dies 2 years later) 5. True
6. True 7. True

MUGGLENET'S EXPERT TRIVIA
PGS. 104-105

1. 11
2. 6
3. Males have stingers, females have suckers
4. Dougal McGregor
5. C. Life in Azkaban
6. Narrow the prediction of when an event will take place
7. D. Parvati Patil
8. A. October 16
9. D. Her great-great-grandmother
10. Hermione

MARAUDER'S MAP **PGS. 106-107**

1. The Hog's Head
2. Hogsmeade
3. The Shrieking Shack
4. The Room of Requirement
5. Hogwarts

YEAR FOUR

DIAGON ALLEY MIX-UP PGS. 110-111

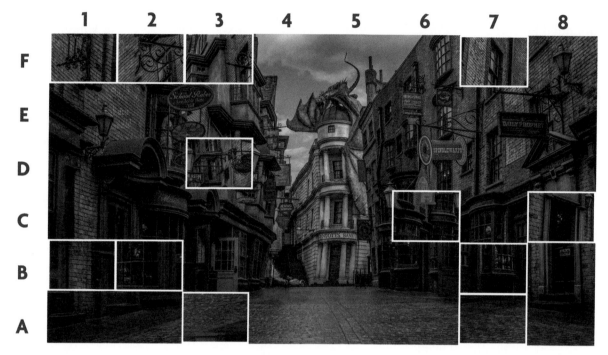

A3: Rotated 180°

A7: Flipped on the vertical axis

B1: Rotated 180°

B2: Flipped on the vertical axis

B7: Flipped on the horizontal axis

C6: Flipped on the vertical axis

C8: Flipped on the vertical axis

D3: Flipped on the vertical axis

F1: Rotated 180°

F2: Flipped on the horizontal axis

F3: Flipped on the vertical axis

F7: Flipped on the vertical axis

THE QUIDDITCH WORLD CUP
PG. 112

1. A. Omnioculars
2. B. Magical Games and Sports
3. C. Dragomir
4. B. 37 Gallons, 15 Sickles and 3 Knuts
5. B. Murphy
6. C. Both A and B
7. Wronski Feint
8. Cover their ears
9. 170, 160

THE CHAMPIONSHIP TEAMS
PG. 114-115

Ireland: McGillicuddy, O'Hara, O'Brian
Bulgaria: Zhukov, Kornova, Nabokov

PROFESSIONAL TEAMS OF BRITAIN AND IRELAND
PG. 116

1. Ballycastle Bats
2. Puddlemere United
3. Montrose Magpies
4. Kenmare Kestrels
5. Tutshill Tornados
6. Pride of Portree
7. Appleby Arrows
8. Caerphilly Catapults
9. Holyhead Harpies
10. Wimbourne Wasps
11. Chudley Cannons
12. Wigtown Wanderers
13. Falmouth Falcons

HOGWARTS CURRICULUM: YEAR FOUR PGS. 118-122

1. A. Four days
2. B. Pulp and Radiohead
3. C. Walden Macnair
4. C. Thomas Riddle Sr. and Mary Riddle
5. A. Not feature Molly Weasley

6. 42 hours
7. *Accio*
8. Banishing Charm
9. *Sonorous*
10. *Morsmordre*
11. *Stupefy*
12. Reductor
13. Bubble-Head
14. *Impedimenta*
15. Four-Point

THE TRIWIZARD MAZE PG. 132

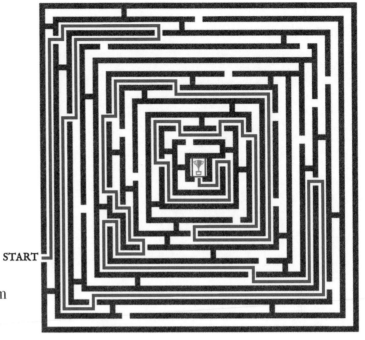

THE WORLD OF WIZARDING SCHOOLS PGS. 124-125

1. Castelobruxo
2. Uagadou
3. Mahoutokoro
4. Ilvermorny
5. Hogwarts
6. Durmstrang
7. Beauxbatons

THE YULE BALL PG. 126

1. C. Parvati Patil
2. F. Padma Patil
3. E. Viktor Krum
4. H. Cho Chang
5. A. Neville Longbottom
6. D. Roger Davies
7. G. Lavender Brown
8. B. Angelina Johnson

TEACHER OF THE YEAR: PROFESSOR MOODY PG. 128

1. C. Both A and B
2. B. Using Transfiguration as punishment
3. B. Pettigrew and Voldemort find him
4. Auror
5. B. After he takes Harry back to the castle
6. Rosier
7. trunk, Imperius
8. C. Twitchy Ears Hex

VOLDEMORT RETURNS PG. 134

1. C. Bone of the father, unknowingly given; flesh of the servant, willingly given; and blood of the enemy, forcibly taken
2. C. White
3. unicorn, snake, Nagini
4. Imperius Curse, bow
5. B. The Lestranges
6. C. Bertha Jorkins
7. *Expelliarmus*
8. A. Lily Potter
9. June 24, 1995
10. C. Spare

THE TRIWIZARD TOURNAMENT PG. 130

The First Task:
1. C. November 24
2. rock, dog
3. C. 4
The Second Task:
1. B. Dobby
2. 45, Cedric Diggory
3. Ron Weasley, Gabrielle Delacour
The Third Task:
1. C. Boggart
2. spider
3. Portkey

MUGGLENET'S EXPERT TRIVIA PG. 137

1. Trans-species transformation
2. Remus Lupin
3. Hippocampus
4. basilisk
5. silver lime
6. Pierre Bonaccord
7. Elladora Ketteridge
8. 1294
9. Edgar Stroulger
10. 1750

LOST IN MUGGLE LONDON
PGS. 140-141

Covent Garden

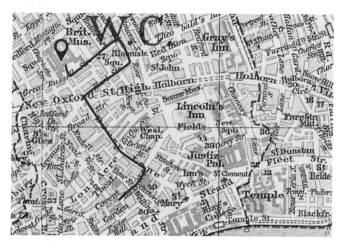

YOUR O.W.L. EXAMS PGS. 142-148

1. B. Switching Spell
2. C. Turns the target into a matchbox
3. A. *Vera Verto*
4. A. Becoming an Animagus
5. D. *Avis*
6. C. Vanishes both animate and inanimate objects
7. B. Aconite
8. C. One month
9. B. Calming Draught
10. B. Firenze
11. Draught of Peace, Properties of Moonstone, Varieties of Venom Antidotes, Strengthening Solution
12. A. Wolfsbane Potion
13. Stag, Jack Russell Terrier, Otter, Horse, Swan, Hare, Fox, Boar
14. *Avada Kedavra, Imperio, Crucio*
15. D. *Incendio*
16. A. *Protego*
17. C. Cassandra
18. live, survives
19. B. 2
20. D. Bone reading
21. A. The Hall of Prophecies
22. B. *Riddikulus*
23. A. Harry saves Dudley and himself from dementors.
    B. Members of the Order of the Phoenix rescue Harry from the Dursleys and take him to Sirius's childhood home.
    C. Harry has his hearing at the Ministry of Magic for using magic outside of Hogwarts.
    D. Harry discovers what has been pulling the seemingly horseless carriages at Hogwarts.
    E. Harry receives his first detention from Umbridge and learns the cost of telling "lies."
    F. Umbridge is appointed High Inquisitor.
    G. Dumbledore's Army holds its first meeting.
    H. Mr. Weasley is attacked by Voldemort's snake while on Order of the Phoenix duty.
    I. Azkaban experiences a mass breakout, which includes the escape of Bellatrix Lestrange.
    J. Hagrid shows Harry and Hermione what he's been hiding in the Forbidden Forest.
    K. Harry, Ron, Hermione, Ginny, Neville and Luna travel to the Department of Mysteries after Harry has a vision of Sirius being tortured by Voldemort there.
    L. Padfoot has his last laugh

THE HEADS OF HOGWARTS
PGS. 150-151

1. C. Dilys Derwent
2. G. Dexter Fortescue
3. J. Everard
4. I. Eupraxia Mole
5. D. Phineas Nigellus Black
6. E. Armando Dippet
7. H. Dolores Umbridge
8. B. Albus Dumbledore
9. A. Severus Snape
10. F. Minerva McGonagall

THE EXPLODING SNAP TEST
PGS. 152-155

3 of Clubs: Each row's two black cards add up to the value of its one red card. Each row has a red card, a club and a spade.

4 of hearts: Each row's first entry is doubled to get the second entry, which is doubled to get the third.

Each row has one black card, one heart and one diamond.

8 of spades: Each row consists of cards of a single color, alternating suits by card. Each row's first card has two subtracted from it to get the second, which has four added to it to get the third.

TEACHER OF THE YEAR: PROFESSOR UMBRIDGE PG. 156

1. A. Senior Undersecretary to the Minister for Magic
2. B. 28
3. Slytherin
4. Draco Malfoy, Vincent Crabbe, Gregory Goyle, Pansy Parkinson, Millicent Bullstrode, Graham Montague, Cassius Warrington
5. C. *Defensive Magical Theory*
6. *Wingardium Leviosa*
7. C. Wands
8. Strengthening Solution
9. Decree 23
10. Decree 22

DECREES OF SEPARATION
PGS. 158-159

Real Decrees: 1, 4, 5, 7, 9

DEMENTORS IN SURREY
PGS. 160-161

START

END

THE MINISTRY OF MAGIC PGS. 162–163

START

END

MUGGLENET'S EXPERT TRIVIA
PG. 164

1. Silvanus Kettleburn
2. Apollyon Pringle
3. ferrets
4. 16
5. Decree 23
6. 53
7. Bubble-Head Charm
8. Invigoration Draught
9. Self-Fertilizing
10. Thestrals

Gary Oldman as Sirius Black and Daniel Radcliffe as Harry Potter in *Harry Potter and the Order of the Phoenix* (2007).

YEAR SIX

THE LOCATION CODE
PGS. 168-169

1. The Burrow
2. Little Hangleton
3. Grimmauld Place
4. Spinner's End
5. Madam Malkin
6. Ollivanders
7. Zonko's
8. Twilfitt and Tatting's

HOGWARTS CURRICULUM: YEAR SIX PGS. 170-174

1. B. Nephew
2. A. The Death Eater battle at the Burrow
3. A. Dumbledore was heterosexual
4. C. Not feature a Defense Against the Dark Arts class
5. A. Dark secrets revealed
6. C. 7,000
7. C. The Defense Against the Dark Arts classroom
8. Rembrandt
9. *Sectumsempra*
10. *Muffliato*
11. *Aguamenti*
12. Argus Filch
13. *Vulnera Sanentur*
14. 1. A. The Other Minister
    2. B. Spinner's End
    3. C. Draco's Detour
    4. G. The Slug Club
    5. E. The House of Gaunt
    6. F. The Unbreakable Vow
    7. D. The Lightning-Struck Tower

PENSIEVE LESSONS PGS. 176-177

1. Little Hangleton
2. Revulsion
3. Parseltongue
4. Hermione
5. You'll go wrong, boy, mark my words
6. Hepzibah Smith

THE HORCRUX CHRONICLES
PGS. 178-179

1. Hogwarts; diary; Ginny Weasley
2. Ring; Marvolo Gaunt; Deathly Hallow
3. Cup; Hufflepuff; Salazar Slytherin
4. Ravenclaw; the Grey Lady; diadem
5. Living; Nagini; Bertha Jorkins; Harry Potter

CODED COMMON ROOM PASSWORDS PGS. 180-183

1. CAPUT DRACONIS
2. MIMBULUS MIMBLETONIA
3. FORTUNA MAJOR
4. FAIRY LIGHTS
5. ODDSBODIKINS
6. BALDERDASH

MUGGLENET'S EXPERT TRIVIA PG. 184

1. Decree 28
2. Toasting her students with a two-handled cup
3. Wilhelmina
4. Crumpets
5. Hiccoughing Solution
6. 1931
7. Kappa
8. *The Standard Book of Spells, Grade Six*
9. Sir Cadogan
10. Daisy Dodderidge

THE NOBLE AND MOST ANCIENT HOUSE OF BLACK
PGS. 186-187

1. Phineas Nigellus
2. Cygnus Black
3. Irma Crabbe
4. Walburga Black
5. Sirius Black
6. Regulus Black
7. Andromeda Black
8. Narcissa Black

THE HALF-BLOOD PRINCE'S TEXTBOOK PGS. 188-189

1. A. Golpalott's Third Law
2. C. *Liberacorpus*
3. D. Severus Snape
4. D. Elixir to Induce Euphoria
5. B. Sunshine
6. C. 5
7. C. Enemies
8. C. Peppermint
9. D. His mother's maiden name
10. A. Ron

Daniel Radcliffe as Harry Potter in *Harry Potter and the Half-Blood Prince* (2009).

THE LIONS OF GRYFFINDOR PGS. 190-191

YEAR SEVEN

THE SEVEN POTTERS PGS. 194-195

1. Hermione Granger
2. Fred Weasley
3. Fleur Delacour
4. Mundungus Fletcher
5. Harry Potter
6. Ron Weasley
7. George Weasley

DUMBLEDORE'S WILL PGS. 196-197

1. Percival, Wulfric, Brian
2. Bilius, Deluminator, remember me
3. Jean, copy, *The Tales of Beedle the Bard*, entertaining, informative
4. James, Snitch, caught, Quidditch match, perseverance, skill

YOUR N.E.W.T. EXAMS PGS. 198-204

1. Food
2. Metamorphosis
3. Into nonbeing
4. Greece
5. *Protego*
6. Undetectable Extension Charm
7. Slughorn
8. *Arresto Momentum*
9. The Hog's Head
10. *Confringo*
11. *Defodio*
12. Dittany
13. Felix Felicis
14. Everlasting elixirs
15. Libatius Borage
16. *Salvio Hexia*
17. Tongue-Tying Curse
18. *Expelliarmus*
19. Peter Pettigrew
20. 200,000

ESCAPE FROM MALFOY MANOR PGS. 206-207

THE TALE OF THE THREE BROTHERS PGS. 208-209

1. *Beedle the Bard*
2. midnight, twilight
3. bridge, river
4. powerful wand, win
5. Resurrection
6. elude, Cloak of Invisibility
7. eight
8. three, veil
9. greeted, old friend, his son

A TRUE GRYFFINDOR

THE UNITED KINGDOM OF MAGIC

1. Platform 9¾
2. Diagon Alley
3. Hogsmeade
4. Hogwarts
5. The Forest of Dean
6. Cokeworth
7. 10 Downing Street
8. Little Whinging, Surrey
9. Godric's Hollow
10. Ottery St. Catchpole

MUGGLENET'S EXPERT TRIVIA

1. Chimeras
2. A fire-breathing chicken
3. 328
4. 11
5. *Obscuro*
6. Undetectable Extension Charm
7. Gemino Curse

CURSED CATCH-UP

1. A. Magical Law Enforcement
2. B. Hermione Granger
3. D. Co-owner of Weasleys' Wizard Wheezes
4. A. Minerva McGonagall
5. A. James Sirius Potter
   B. Albus Severus Potter
   C. Lily Luna Potter
   D. Rose Granger-Weasley
   E. Scorpius Malfoy

MATCH THE WAND MOVEMENT

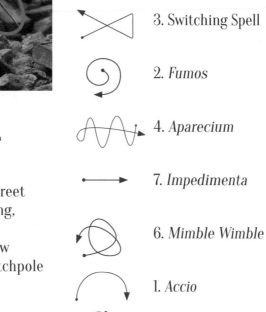

3. Switching Spell

2. *Fumos*

4. *Aparecium*

7. *Impedimenta*

6. *Mimble Wimble*

1. *Accio*

5. *Alohomora*

Daniel Radcliffe as Harry Potter leading his cohort into the Lestrange vault at Gringotts in *Harry Potter and the Deathly Hallows: Part 1* (2010).

NEWT'S CASE

PGS. 220-221

START

END

A WALK AROUND WIZARDING NEW YORK **PGS. 222-223**

START

END